AQA Spanish
Grammar & Translation Workbook

A LEVEL AND AS

Vincent Everett

OXFORD
UNIVERSITY PRESS

Great Clarendon Street, Oxford, OX2 6DP, United Kingdom

Oxford University Press is a department of the University of Oxford.
It furthers the University's objective of excellence in research,
scholarship, and education
by publishing worldwide. Oxford is a registered trade
mark of Oxford University Press in the UK and in certain other
countries.

© Oxford University Press 2017

The moral rights of the author have been asserted.

First published in 2017

British Library Cataloguing in Publication Data

Data available

978-0-19-841555-8

13

Paper used in the production of this book is a natural, recyclable
product made from wood grown in
sustainable forests.

The manufacturing process conforms to the environmental
regulations of the country of origin.

Printed in China by Shanghai Offset Printing Products Ltd

Cover photograph: Jean-Pierre Lescourret/Getty Images

Illustrations: Aptara

Contents

Introduction

Grammar and translation in the AQA exams

Each of the papers in the AS and A Level exams will measure your ability to manipulate language accurately, using a range of structures, with a specific mark awarded for quality of language. A sound grasp of the grammar points that appear in the specification lists is therefore essential.

For the AS exam you will need to be able to translate 70 words from Spanish into English and from English into Spanish, with content based on the specification themes and sub-themes. For A Level this will be 100 words.

How to use this book

The grammar transition section at the start of this book will help you bridge the gap between GCSE and AS/A Level, or refresh the basics at the start of A Level Year 2. There may be particular areas where you are lacking confidence or which you wish to revise.

The remainder of the book is divided into four sections, with the order of grammar points generally reflecting the order in which they are covered in OUP's AQA Spanish AS/A Level Year 1 and A Level Year 2 Student Books. This is to allow students who are using these books to practise as they go along, reinforcing what has been learned in the classroom with further activities at home. Alternatively you may wish to focus on areas of particular difficulty or work through a particular section as part of your revision plan.

Grammar practice

Each page in this section focuses on a specific grammar point, some of which are returned to and developed throughout the book. Different activities will test your ability to recognise and to apply particular rules and structures, with grammar and tip boxes to help you.

Mixed practice

Once you've covered all the grammar points in one section, you're ready for the mixed practice activities. These allow you to practise the grammar points you've been working on without additional guidance, preparing you to apply the structures confidently and fluently in the exams.

Translation practice

Each section ends with four pages of translation practice, divided into two pages of Spanish to English translation, and two pages of English to Spanish translation. The first page of each pair practises translating short phrases and expressions, with additional hints and tips. The second page features three passages to translate, each between 70 and 100 words. The vocabulary and themes covered are based around the AS Level specification, with some inclusion of A Level themes for the 100-word passages.

Additional features

Gramática	**Consejo**
Grammar boxes offer a concise explanation of the point being covered.	Tip boxes offer extra 'handy hints' for tackling different questions, for remembering particular rules and for approaching translation activities.

⭐ Activities marked with a star cover grammar you may be expected to produce in an exam at A Level Year 2 only.

Verb tables and answers are supplied at the back of the book.

1 **Which rule would these nouns exemplify? Choose the correct number from the list in the grammar box.**

a un problema __

b un español __

c un turista / una periodista __

d una moto __

e la gente __

f los jardines __

g una modelo __

h los robots __

2 **Underline the feminine nouns and circle the masculine ones.**

> tema   nacionalidad   intenciones   foto
> túnel   paisaje   socialista

3 **Make these nouns plural.**

a hotel _____

b preocupación _____

c inglés _____

d sistema _____

e cuarto de baño _____

4 **Circle the eight errors and write the correct option below.**

Una problema es que las gentes van a hotels en la costa de españa y no respetan el naturaleza. No solo en los ciudades, sino en toda la costa hay edificios grandes muy cerca de la mar. Cuando vamos de vacacions tenemos que considerar el efecto en el medio ambiente.

_____   _____

_____   _____

_____   _____

_____   _____

5 **Complete the translation into Spanish.**

Spanish people wear fashionable clothes and shoes. In the photo we can see Inés, who is a model as well as a journalist. She works for an organisation which promotes companies from Spain throughout Europe.

Los ᵃ _____ llevan ᵇ _____

y ᶜ _____ a la moda. En ᵈ _____

_____ vemos a Inés que es

ᵉ _____ además de ᶠ _____.

Trabaja para ᵍ _____ _____ que promociona a

empresas españolas por toda Europa.

Gramática

Read through these rules for Spanish nouns.

i Words ending in *-o* are often masculine. Words ending in *-a* are often feminine.

ii There are some exceptions where a word ending in *-o* is a shortened version of a feminine word.

iii These endings tend to be masculine: *-ema, -ama, -or, -ín, -el, -al, -aje*.

iv These endings tend to be feminine: *-tud, -dad, -ción, -sión, -itis*.

v Words ending in *-ista* can be masculine or feminine depending on the person.

vi Some words look masculine but often refer to a woman, so have become feminine.

vii Plurals are formed by adding an *-s* to words ending in a vowel, or *-es* to a consonant.

viii For words ending in *-n* or *-s* with an accent on the last vowel, the accent is removed in the plural form.

ix Some nouns which are usually plural in English are singular in Spanish.

x Nouns of nationality do not have a capital letter.

xi Some words which have come into Spanish via another language don't follow the Spanish rules.

1 Look at the examples and complete the rule for the correct formation of the adjective.

> **Gramática**
>
> In Spanish, adjectives have to match the noun they describe for gender and singular/plural.

a precioso → preciosa

If an adjective ends in an -o, to make it feminine _____.

b importante (m), importante (f)

If an adjective doesn't end in an -o as in the example in a) above, the ending for the feminine and the masculine form _____.

c acogedor → acogedora

For the ending -or _____.

d francés → francesa

Some adjectives of nationality end in a stressed vowel in the masculine form, but in the feminine form _____.

e rápido → rápidos

To make an adjective plural, if it ends in a vowel _____.

f natural → naturales

If it ends in a consonant, _____ to make it plural.

g eficaz → eficaces

Words ending in -z _____ in the plural form.

h una página *web* → unas páginas *web*

Some adjectives that have come into Spanish from English _____.

2 Write the correct form of these adjectives.

a trabajador → feminine plural _____

b interesante → feminine singular _____

c difícil → feminine plural _____

d cariñoso → masculine plural _____

e alemán → feminine singular _____

f feliz → feminine plural _____

g web → masculine plural _____

3 Put the adjective into the correct form.

a Las familias _____ ya no son tan _____ como antes. (*español, tradicional*)

b Los jóvenes de hoy son _____ y _____. (*serio, trabajador*)

c La tecnología _____ es muy _____. Hay unos sitios _____ para todo.

(*moderno, útil, web*)

d Los mayores son muy _____. (*capaz*)

4 Explain the difference between these two sets of sentences.

a **i** En mi familia tengo un hermano y una hermana muy inteligente.

ii En mi familia tengo un hermano y una hermana muy inteligentes.

_____

_____

b **i** Hay una profesora de español y un profesor de dibujo muy trabajadores.

ii Hay una profesora de español y un profesor de dibujo muy trabajador.

_____

_____

1 Insert the correct definite article.

a Veía un programa en _____ televisión.

b _____ programa era muy bueno.

c _____ profesores hablan español.

d En _____ aula hay una pizarra interactiva.

e Tengo alergia a _____ mariscos.

f _____ bronquitis es muy grave.

g Cogí el autobús de _____ centro a mi casa.

h Fui a _____ cine con mis amigos.

2 Decide on the correct indefinite article.

a Veía _____ programa en la television.

b Hay _____ programas muy buenos.

c Mi primo tiene _____ resfríado.

d Viven en _____ casa muy grande.

e Compraron _____ piso pequeño.

f Es _____ ciudad muy aislada.

g Quiero ser _____ periodista.

3 Complete the translation into Spanish using the correct article.

The dentist worked in a surgery near the centre of the town. She was a rich and important member of society. In the waiting room was a student who needed help. She had a toothache, but she also had a much greater problem.

ᵃ_____ dentista trabajaba en ᵇ _____ consultorio cerca ᶜ _____ centro de

ᵈ _____ ciudad. Era ᵉ _____ miembro rico e importante de ᶠ _____

sociedad. En ᵍ _____ sala de espera había ʰ _____ estudiante que

necesitaba ayuda. Le dolía ⁱ _____ muela, pero también tenía ʲ _____

problema mucho mayor.

4 Decide which two words from the list could grammatically fit in each gap (think of the gender and number). Then decide from the context which one makes most sense. Check your answers using a dictionary.

La mayoría de las ᵃ _____ viven en un

ᵇ _____ en un ᶜ _____ grande.

Se puede subir por las ᵈ _____ o en uno de los

ᵉ _____. En la ᶠ _____ hay unos

ᵍ _____ para llamar, así que te pueden abrir la

ʰ _____ sin necesidad de bajar.

familias	timbres
piso	calle
edificio	escaleras
puerta	ascensores

⊞ Gramática

The definite article 'the' has four forms in Spanish:

el (masculine singular)
la (feminine singular)
los (masculine plural)
las (feminine plural)

Feminine words which begin with *a* and where the stress falls on the initial *a*, take *el* instead of *la*, but are still feminine, e.g. *El agua está fría.* (The water is cold.)

Spanish often uses a definite article where English would not:

Me gusta el chocolate.

Me gustan las matemáticas y el inglés.

When *el* comes after *a* (at/to) or *de* (of/from), it changes to *al* and *del*.

Revise the typical endings for masculine and feminine nouns on page 5.

⊞ Gramática

In Spanish the indefinite article 'a/an' has two forms: *un* (masculine) and *una* (feminine).

There is also a plural form for 'some': *unos* (masculine) and *unas* (feminine).

Feminine words which begin with a stressed *a* take *un* instead of *una*, but are still feminine, e.g. *un aula vacía* (an empty classroom).

When a job or profession is preceded by the verb *ser*, the indefinite article is not always required, e.g. *Soy artista.* (I am an artist.)

1 Translate a–e into Spanish. Check the rules of adjectival agreement on page 6.

a She has a very fast computer.

_____

b I live in a modern house.

_____

c There are beautiful views.

_____

d She has generous parents.

_____

e I went to a birthday party.

_____

> **Gramática**
>
> In Spanish it is normal to put the noun first, followed by the adjective, e.g. *un ejemplo corto*.

2 What is the difference between the two sentences? Use a separate sheet of paper for your answers.

a **i** Este es mi antiguo instituto.

  ii Asistí a un instituto muy antiguo.

b **i** Son muy grandes amigos.

  ii Tiene un amigo muy grande.

c **i** ¡Mis pobres padres!

  ii Viene de una familia pobre.

d **i** Fue mi única experiencia.

  ii Fue una experiencia única.

e **i** Para beber había pura agua.

  ii Para beber había agua pura.

> **Gramática**
>
> Some adjectives can move in front of the noun and change their meaning.
>
> *Compré un nuevo coche.* (I bought a new car.) (New to me, but not necessarily brand new.)
>
> *Tengo un coche nuevo.* (I have a brand new car.)

3 Read these sentences with examples of apocopation. What is the full form of the adjective? Write the adjective next to the sentence.

a Vivo en el tercer piso. _____

b Es un muy buen ejemplo. _____

c ¿Algún alumno está enfermo? _____

d No hay ningún problema. _____

e Hace muy mal tiempo. _____

> **Gramática**
>
> Some adjectives move in front of a masculine singular noun and have a shortened form. This is called apocopation.
>
> *primero → primer*
> *mi primer amor* (my first love)
>
> The word *grande* can shorten in front of feminine and masculine singular nouns:
>
> *un gran amigo / una gran amiga* (a great friend)

> ✅ **Consejo**
>
> To remember this, think of what happens to the word *uno*. It shortens to *un* whenever it is directly in front of a masculine singular noun.

4 Write the correct form of the adjective in the correct place in the sentence.

a Es una ciudad. (*precioso*) _____

b Es una ciudad. (*muy antiguo*) _____

c Es un amigo y una persona. (*grande, bueno*) _____

d Es un amigo y una persona. (*bueno, grande*) _____

e Es una amiga y una persona. (*grande, bueno*) _____

f Es una amiga y una persona. (*bueno, grande*) _____

1 Look at these verbs in the present tense. Complete the grid.

	-ar/-er/-ir?	Person?	Meaning in English
vivimos			
escribís			
nada			
estudias			
escogéis			
bebemos			

2 Translate these sentences into English.

a Preferimos pasar las vacaciones en Inglaterra. _____

_____

b Viven en España. _____

c Mi madre me llama por teléfono cada día. _____

_____

d Bebes demasiado. _____

e Mis hermanos deciden donde comemos. _____

_____

3 Put the verb into the specified person in the present tense in Spanish, then translate it into English.

a nadar (*1st plural*) _____

b visitar (*1st singular*) _____

c ayudar (*2nd plural*) _____

d salir (*3rd singular*) _____

e poner (*2nd singular*) _____

f olvidar (*3rd plural*) _____

g abrir (*1st singular*) _____

h hacer (*3rd plural*) _____

> **⊞ Gramática**
>
> Some common irregular verbs have a *g* in the 1st person singular only.
>
> *tener → tengo*
>
> Some infinitives ending in *-cer/-cir* have irregular 1st person singular forms with *z*.
>
> *conocer → conozco*

4 Write out the correct form of the 1st person singular in the present tense.

hacer _____   traer _____

poner _____   conducir _____

decir _____   padecer _____

venir _____   ofrecer _____

salir _____   crecer _____

caer _____   establecer _____

> **⊞ Gramática**
>
> To conjugate verbs in the present tense, add the correct ending for
>
> 1st person (I)
>
> 2nd person (you)
>
> 3rd person (he, she, it)
>
> 1st person plural (we)
>
> 2nd person plural (you)
>
> 3rd person plural (they).
>
> The formal form of 'you', *usted* or *ustedes*, takes the 3rd person endings.
>
> Regular verbs follow the present tense pattern in the verb tables on page 84.

✅ Consejo

Look at the verb tables on page 84 and find the endings for regular verbs in the preterite tense.

1a What do you notice about the endings for the 1st and 3rd person singular ('I' and 'he/she/it') in the preterite tense?

_____

1b Compare the endings of the 1st person plural ('we') for present and preterite. What do you notice?

_____

2 Match the English to the Spanish.

a	decidí	i	he decided
b	jugó	ii	we swam
c	nadaron	iii	he played
d	decidieron	iv	they played
e	jugaron	v	they decided
f	nadamos	vi	I decided
g	decidió	vii	they swam

3 Underline the verbs in the preterite. Translate them into English.

Ese día llegó tarde al instituto. Los otros alumnos trabajaban en silencio y lo miraron asustados cuando entró de repente. 'Lo siento,' murmuró y sacó sus cuadernos y empezó a trabajar.

_____

_____

4 Now translate this version into Spanish, being careful with the 1st person forms.

That day I arrived late to school. The other students were working in silence and they looked at me surprised when I came in suddenly. 'I'm sorry,' I murmured and I took out my exercise books and started to work.

_____

_____

_____

_____

_____

🔲 Gramática

The preterite tense is used for saying what happened. It is for actions performed in a specific completed time frame in the past. (Compare this to the definition of the imperfect tense on page 11.)

🔲 Gramática

Infinitives ending in -gar, -car or -zar change spelling in the 1st person to match the pronunciation:

jugar → ju**gu**é (**not** jugé)

sacar → sa**qu**é (**not** sacé)

comenzar → comen**c**é (**not** comenzé)

✅ Consejo

You may have seen some examples of strong preterite verbs:

tener → tuve

decir → dije

You will find more on these on page 19.

1 Translate these sentences into English.

a   Mis abuelos vivían en un pueblo pequeño. _____
_____

b   Mis padres odiaban vivir lejos de la ciudad. _____
_____

c   Mi padre iba a la escuela todos los días. _____
_____

d   Mi madre ayudaba con las tareas domésticas. _____
_____

2 Complete the sentences with the verb in the correct form of the imperfect tense.

a   Mi hermana _____ en el instituto. (*comer*)

b   Yo _____ en casa. (*comer*)

c   Todos los días yo _____ mis deberes. (*hacer*)

d   Después mi hermana y yo _____ al futból. (*jugar*)

e   Mis padres _____ hasta muy tarde. (*trabajar*)

3 Which of these verbs are in the imperfect? Underline them and give the English translation.

Vivía con mis padres y no me gustaba porque tenía que pedir permiso para
todo. Un día invité a mi novia a comer cuando mis padres no estaban, y me
regañaron. Nunca me permitían hacer nada.

_____

_____

4 Read these sentences in English. Circle the verbs that need to be put into
the imperfect. Underline the verbs that need to go into the preterite. Then
translate the text into Spanish.

We were living in Mexico and everything was very different. My brother used
to go out and see his friends, but I had to stay at home. One day my friends
were going to go to the cinema and I decided to go as well. My mum was not
happy but she did not say anything to my dad.

_____

_____

_____

_____

_____

_____

_____

_____

_____

⬚ Gramática

The imperfect tense is used for saying
what was happening or what used
to happen. It is for repeated actions
or describing ongoing actions over a
period of time.

Watch out for English using the simple
past or even the conditional when it is
really something that used to happen:

When I was young I would swim in the
river. *Cuando era joven nadaba en el río.*

When I was young I played tennis all
the time. *Cuando era joven jugaba al
tenis todo el tiempo.*

Look at the verb tables on page 84 for
the endings in the imperfect tense.

Only three verbs are irregular in the
imperfect tense:

ser → era

ir → iba

ver → veía

1a The formation of the conditional is different from all the other tenses you have learnt so far. What is the first thing you normally do when conjugating a verb, and which you must not do for the conditional?

_____

1b Look at the endings and compare them to endings in other tenses. What do they look the same as?

_____

1c Compare the conditional for -ar, -er and -ir verbs. What do you notice?

_____

2 Translate these conditional verbs into English.

a   viviríamos _____

b   irían _____

c   me casaría _____

d   mi hermano compraría _____

e   ganarías _____

3 Find out what happens to these verbs in the conditional. Add them to your grammar reference notes.

salir	decir	saber	valer
tener	venir	haber	querer
poner	hacer	poder	caber

4 Put these verbs into the specified form in the conditional.

a   _____ al balonmano. (*jugar, nosotros*)

b   _____ que ayudar. (*tener, yo*)

c   _____ ir también. (*poder, ella*)

d   Nos _____ vivir en España. (*gustar*)

e   Mi hermano _____ contigo. (*salir*)

5 Translate this text into Spanish.

I would like to live in a city. I would go to the cinema every day and I would see all the new films. I would go shopping and I would buy beautiful clothes. I would invite my friends and we would eat in expensive restaurants. I would work in a bank and I would earn lots of money. My parents would come and live nearby.

_____

_____

_____

_____

_____

_____

Gramática

The conditional is used to talk about what **would** happen:

Me gustaría (I would like)

Nadaría (I would swim)

Consejo

Look at the verb endings for regular verbs in the conditional on page 84.

Gramática

All verbs have the same endings in the conditional. Some verbs do have an irregular stem. Many of these are the same verbs which take a *g* in the 1st person of the present tense.

salir → saldría

This makes them easier to pronounce.

But watch out: verbs like *preferiría* do not get shortened; you just have to say them carefully.

1 **Write these sentences in the future tense.**

a Trabajo en una fábrica.

_____

b Mi hermano es abogado.

_____

c Tenemos una casa en la playa.

_____

d Mis padres vienen a visitarme.

_____

e Puedes visitarme también.

_____

> **⚑ Gramática**
>
> The future tense is used to talk about what will happen.
>
> _iré_ (I will go)
>
> _será_ (it will be)
>
> The future tense has the same stem as the conditional tense (see page 12).
>
> Look at the verb tables on page 84 and note the endings for the future tense.

> **✅ Consejo**
>
> Remember that the verbs which have an irregular stem in the conditional have the same irregular stem in the future tense.

2 **Translate this text into Spanish.**

In the future things will be different. We will have robots to do all the work. They will make our life easy. We will live 1000 years because they will transfer our personality to a disc.

_____

_____

_____

_____

_____

3 **Match the sentence halves.**

a	Mis padres	**i**	va a estudiar español.
b	Mi amigo	**ii**	voy a sacar buenas notas.
c	Yo	**iii**	van a comprar una casa en España.
d	Mis amigos y yo	**iv**	vamos en un viaje escolar.
e	¿Tú	**v**	vais a venir?
f	¿Vosotros	**vi**	vas a hacer los deberes conmigo?

> **⚑ Gramática**
>
> Another way to talk about the future is to use the correct part of the verb _ir_ (to go) followed by an infinitive.
>
> _Voy a hablar._ (I am going to talk.)
>
> _Va a jugar._ (She is going to play.)
>
> With a reflexive verb you have a choice of where to put the reflexive pronoun.
>
> It can go on the end of the infinitive:
>
> _Voy a vestirme._ (I am going to get dressed.)
>
> It can go in front of the verb 'to go':
>
> _Me voy a vestir._ (I am going to get dressed.)

4 **Rewrite the text from activity 2 in Spanish using 'going to' instead of the future tense.**

_____

_____

_____

_____

_____

1 **Match the Spanish with the English.**

a No tengo ganas de ir al partido de fútbol.

b Acabo de llegar.

c Estoy a punto de hacer mis deberes.

d Va a empezar a llover.

e Me voy a poner a llorar.

f Me ayuda a hacer los deberes.

g Voy a dejar de ir al entrenamiento de fútbol.

h No vuelvo a ir a un partido de fútbol.

i I am going to give up going to football training.

ii She helps me to do my homework.

iii I'm going to start to cry.

iv I don't feel like going to the football match.

v I have just arrived.

vi It is going to start to rain.

vii I'm not going to go to a football match again.

viii I am about to do my homework.

⚑ Gramática

These verbs are followed by the infinitive.

tener que (to have to)

poder (to be able to)

deber (should)

querer (to want)

necesitar (to need)

esperar (to hope)

saber (to know how to)

intentar (to try)

evitar (to avoid)

lograr (to manage to)

soler (to usually do something)

---

2 **Translate these expressions into English.**

a tener ganas de _____

b acabar de _____

c estar a punto de _____

d ponerse a _____

e comenzar a _____

f ayudar a _____

g dejar de _____

h volver a _____

☑ Consejo

Many of these verbs followed by the infinitive are radical changing verbs. See page 15 for more practice.

☑ Consejo

In Spanish, if an infinitive is in the middle of a sentence and isn't part of one of these infinitive constructions, you may need to use *para*.

Voy a ir a España para ver a mis abuelos. (I am going to go to Spain in order to see my grandparents.)

⚑ Gramática

Negative words are often used together with *no*.

No he comido nada. (I haven't eaten anything.)

No conozco a nadie. (I don't know anyone.)

Or they can go at the beginning of the sentence, without a *no*.

Nadie me ayuda. (Nobody helps me.)

Nunca hace sus deberes. (He never does his homework.)

nada (nothing)

nadie (nobody)

ni … ni … (neither … nor …)

ninguno (not one)

nunca (never)

tampoco (neither)

ni siquiera (not even)

---

3 **Rewrite these sentences using the same negative expression in the alternative way – see the grammar box to help you.**

a Nada me gusta en esa tienda. _____

b Tampoco tienen buenos precios. _____

c Ni tienen buen servicio ni buenos productos. _____

d No tienen ni siquiera unos empleados informados. _____

e No te ayuda nadie. _____

f Nunca voy a volver a comprar cosas allí. _____

1 Compara estos verbos con el infinitivo. Identifica el cambio de raíz subrayando la sílaba a la que afecta.

prefiero	quieren	puedes	requiere	mantienen
preferir	querer	poder	requerir	mantener

2 Escribe el infinitivo de estos verbos.

a tiene _____

b juego _____

c vuelven _____

d pide _____

e viene _____

f duermen _____

3 Traduce al español e indica si necesitan cambiar su raíz o no.

a we want _____

b they require _____

c we maintain _____

d we play _____

e I sleep _____

f we prefer _____

g he returns _____

4 Cambia este texto de la primera persona del singular (*yo*), a la primera persona del plural (*nosotros*).

Paso mucho tiempo hablando por el teléfono móvil. Juego con los videojuegos, escucho música y prefiero salir siempre con el teléfono. Lo utilizo todo el tiempo, por ejemplo si quiero saber algo, lo busco en Internet.

_____

_____

_____

_____

5 Completa el texto con verbos en el presente. Decide si el verbo cambia su raíz o no.

Luís Suárez (*jugar*) ᵃ _____ como delantero. (*Marcar*)

ᵇ _____ muchos goles y (*perder*) ᶜ _____

muy pocos partidos. (*Tener*) ᵈ _____ mala fama porque a

veces (*morder*) ᵉ _____ a miembros del equipo contrario.

(*Representar*) ᶠ _____ un papel negativo de este deporte

porque quizás (*soler*) ᵍ _____ ser muy competitivo. Pero

nosotros no (*poder*) ʰ _____ criticar a Suárez sin reconocer

que (*tener*) ⁱ _____ mucho talento.

Gramática

Many verbs change their stem in the present tense. The stem changes in the 1st, 2nd and 3rd persons singular, and in the 3rd person plural. The forms for 'we' and 'you' plural do not change.

e.g.

*po*der: *pue*do   *pue*des   *pue*de
*po*demos   *po*déis   *pue*den

Sometimes a radical changing verb may have an irregular first person singular form, e.g. *tengo*.

1 Escribe la forma correcta del pronombre reflexivo en el lugar adecuado. No todos los espacios necesitan un pronombre.

a   Los chicos también maquillan.

b   Las chicas a veces afeitan.

c   No acuesto antes de terminar el trabajo.

d   Es importante lavar los dientes.

2 Escribe la forma correcta del verbo entre paréntesis.

a   Leonardo _____ con mi prima. (*casarse*)

b   Debemos _____ de nuestras responsabilidades. (*acordarse*)

c   Mis hijos _____ muy temprano. (*levantarse*)

d   ¿Cómo _____ dentro de diez años? (*imaginarse, tú*)

e   Mis padres _____ . (*divorciarse*)

3 Subraya los verbos reflexivos en este texto.

Cuando hablamos de los participantes del cambio social es importante que nos incluyamos como ejemplos de cómo las cosas se transforman de generación a generación. Te inspiras quizás en los héroes que se enfrentaron al racismo y al sexismo, pero no nos podemos permitir pensar que la lucha se ha terminado.

4 Compara el texto en inglés. Utiliza los diferentes usos a–f (ver el cuadro de gramática) para explicar en cada caso por qué se necesita un verbo reflexivo.

When we talk about the participants in social change it is important to include ourselves as examples of how things change from generation to generation. You are inspired perhaps by the heroes who faced up to racism and sexism, but we can't allow ourselves to think that the struggle has ended.

5 Subraya en este texto los verbos que necesitan la forma reflexiva. Luego traduce el texto al español utilizando el vocabulario.

The number of Spanish people who get married reduces every year. A family is not defined by marriage. Many people live together without getting married, but they still love each other.

_____

_____

_____

_____

Gramática

Reflexive verbs are used for actions we do to ourselves, e.g.

lavarse (to wash oneself)
sentarse (to sit oneself down)

The reflexive pronoun needs to match the person of the verb:

me *levanto* (I get myself up)
nos *vestimos* (we dress ourselves)

The reflexive pronouns are:

me	nos
te	os
se	se

The reflexive pronoun goes on the end of the infinitive: *levantarse* or in front of the conjugated verb: *me levanto*.

Gramática

Look out for the different times a reflexive verb is required in Spanish:

a   When English would also use 'myself': I hurt myself – *me lastimé*

b   Where English would use the word 'get': to get dressed – to dress yourself – *vestirse*

c   Where English would say 'each other': they hate each other – *se odian*

d   Where in English 'self' is implied but not used: to shut (oneself) up – *callarse*

e   Where in English you would use the passive: it is recognised that – it recognises itself that – *se reconoce que*

f   There are some verbs you just have to remember are reflexive in Spanish: to stay – *quedarse*

número	definir
españoles	el matrimonio
reducir	convivir
cada	de todas maneras

1 Empareja el español (a–d) con el inglés (i–iv).

a me gusta   **i** they like it

b les gusta   **ii** he likes them

c le gustan   **iii** we liked it

d nos gustó   **iv** I like

2 Traduce al inglés.

a A los jóvenes les interesa mucho. _____

_____

b A mis padres les molesta. _____

_____

c Me encantaba. _____

d No nos importa. _____

e Me importas mucho. _____

f Me duelen los pies. _____

> **✓ Consejo**
>
> If you're uncertain of how to translate the pronouns in activity 3, you can check the formation of indirect pronouns in the grammar box on page 36.

3 Traduce al español.

a My parents don't like it. _____

b Young people don't mind it. _____

c You worry me. _____

d They love it. _____

e We don't like tomatoes. _____

4 Subraya donde se requiere el uso de un verbo impersonal en español.

Young people think that it is important to work hard. It is important to them to have a good job and they love to earn money. Saving the planet does not worry them.

5 Traduce el texto al español utilizando el vocabulario de abajo.

_____

_____

_____

_____

_____

los jóvenes	un trabajo
importante	ganar dinero
trabajar duro	salvar el planeta

Gramática

The most common impersonal verb in Spanish is *gustar*.

Me gusta does not literally mean 'I like'. It means 'it is pleasing to me'.

Other verbs that work in a similar way are:

me importa

me encanta

me molesta

me interesa

me preocupa

me duele

The verb ending can change:

me gustas (you please me – I like you)

me gustan las flores (flowers please me – I like flowers)

me gustó (it pleased me – I liked it)

The pronoun can change:

le gusta (it is pleasing to him – he likes it)

Because *le gusta* means 'it is pleasing to him/to her', when you include the subject of the sentence, you have to start with *a…* ('to…').

a mi hermano le gusta (to my brother it is pleasing – my brother likes)

a mi hermana no le importa (to my sister it doesn't matter – my sister doesn't mind)

1 Subraya los verbos en tiempos continuos. Luego tradúcelos al inglés.

En 2006 estaba viviendo en España y estaba trabajando en una empresa de construcción. Cuando llegó la crisis económica perdí mi trabajo y volví a mi país. Ahora estoy viviendo en Marruecos y estoy ganando más dinero que cuando vivía en España.

_____

_____

_____

_____

2 Utiliza el vocabulario de la actividad 1 para traducir las frases al español.

a My company is losing money.

_____

b I am returning to Spain.

_____

c I was working in Morocco.

_____

d I am arriving in my country.

_____

> ✅ **Consejo**
>
> Remember that *ser* never takes the continuous tense.

3 Cambia los verbos a la forma continua.

a Mi hermana vive en Túnez.

_____

b Ella trabajaba en la agricultura.

_____

c Hoy trabaja en la construcción.

_____

d Construyen un pueblo nuevo.

_____

4 Traduce al español.

After working in Morocco, he is now living in Spain. Instead of working in construction, he is working in agriculture. He was building a new town and although they are still building the town, he is not working there.

_____

_____

_____

_____

🔧 Gramática

As well as the simple present, Spanish also has a continuous form of the present.

Present continuous: *estoy nadando* (I am swimming)

The present continuous is always formed with *estar* plus the present participle.

The present participle of regular -*ar* verbs is formed with -*ando*: *hablando* (talking).

For -*er* and -*ir* verbs it is formed with -*iendo*: *comiendo* (eating).

Some verbs have a spelling change: *leer → leyendo*, *ir → yendo*.

Any -*ir* verb which is a radical changing verb has an irregular stem for the present participle: *preferir → prefiriendo*.

🔧 Gramática

There is also an alternative continuous form of the imperfect tense.

estaba nadando (I was swimming)

estaba comiendo (I was eating)

See page 11 for the imperfect tense.

✅ Consejo

Do not be tempted to use the present participle in sentences where English uses the '-ing' form but Spanish requires the infinitive.

I like to swim/I like swimming – *Me gusta nadar*

Instead of swimming – *En vez de nadar*

After swimming – *Después de nadar*

The only exception is in the construction *seguir* + present participle:

sigue siendo (it carries on being)

✅ Consejo

The simple present tense in Spanish can also be used to translate the English continuous form.

nado todos los días (I swim every day)

nado en este momento (I am swimming now)

See page 9 for the present tense.

1 Empareja estos verbos con el infinitivo. Traduce los verbos a–j al inglés poniendo atención en la persona correcta.

a	dije	**i**	querer	_____	
b	quiso	**ii**	poner	_____	
c	puso	**iii**	poder	_____	
d	pudieron	**iv**	traer	_____	
e	trajimos	**v**	hacer	_____	
f	hicieron	**vi**	estar	_____	
g	estuve	**vii**	saber	_____	
h	supieron	**viii**	venir	_____	
i	vine	**ix**	decir	_____	
j	cupo	**x**	caber	_____	

2 Pon el verbo en la forma correcta del pretérito.

a tener _____ (yo)

b hacer _____ (nosotros)

c decir _____ (ellos)

d traer _____ (ella)

e estar _____ (vosotros)

f poder _____ (tú)

g poner _____ (nosotros)

h saber _____ (yo)

3 Identifica y traduce los cinco verbos en el pretérito fuerte.

Vinieron mis primos a mi fiesta y provocaron varios problemas. Bebieron demasiado y salieron al parking a discutir. Hicieron mucho ruido y cuando quisieron volver a la fiesta no pudieron porque mi tío (su padre) dijo que no.

a _____

b _____

c _____

d _____

e _____

4 Traduce al español utilizando el vocabulario.

My uncle and aunt didn't come to my party. They were able to send me a present. I said I understood, but they didn't make much of an effort.

mandar	un regalo	entender	un esfuerzo

_____

_____

_____

🔧 Gramática

The strong preterite

Some verbs have a different form in the preterite tense. As a group they are referred to as the 'strong preterite'.

They have slightly different endings to regular preterite tense verbs:

tener: tuve tuviste tuvo
tuvimos tuvisteis tuvieron

These endings apply to -ar, -er and -ir strong preterite verbs, and do not have the normal preterite tense accents.

The strong preterite stem is different from the infinitive so you need to learn them:

tener – tuve

querer – quise

decir – dije

There are some spelling changes for pronunciation:

hacer – hice hiciste hizo

Where the stem ends in a _j_, there is no _i_ in the third person plural: _dijeron, trajeron_.

See page 10 for the regular preterite tense.

🔧 Gramática

Some of these strong preterite verbs have a slightly different meaning when used in this tense.

Imperfect: _Podía comprar un ordenador o una tableta_ (I was able to/could)

Preterite: _Pude comprar un ordenador_ (I managed to, was able to and did)

Imperfect: _Quería abrir la puerta_ (I wanted to)

Preterite: _Quise abrir la puerta_ (I tried to, I wanted to, but couldn't)

Imperfect: _Tenía una idea_ (I had)

Preterite: _Tuve una idea_ (It came to me, I thought of)

Imperfect: _Sabía quién era_ (I knew)

Preterite: _Supe quién era_ (I found out/realised)

1 Escribe la traducción en inglés al lado de los dibujos de abajo.

a Aquí se habla español.

b El desayuno se sirve a las siete.

c No se permite correr.

d Se recicla el vidrio.

e Se busca, vivo o muerto.

f Se vende.

> **Gramática**
>
> English often uses the passive voice ('dinner is served'). In Spanish it is very common to avoid the use of the passive voice by using the reflexive pronoun *se*: It is made in England – *Se hace en Inglaterra.*

2 Lee y decide qué se describe.

a Se juega con dos equipos. Se gana cuando después de noventa minutos un equipo marca más goles. No se puede tocar el balón con la mano. _____

b Se conectan al ordenador y se utilizan para escuchar música. Se pueden encontrar unos que son inalámbricos. _____

c Se requiere para poder conducir. Se consigue oficialmente después de hacer un examen. Se tiene que hacer un examen práctico y otro teórico.

_____

3 En los textos de la actividad 2, subraya todos los verbos con *se*. Tradúcelos al inglés.

Ejemplo: *Se juega* – it is played

_____
_____
_____
_____
_____
_____
_____

4 Traduce al español.

It is played with a ball. It is not permitted to touch the ball with your feet. Points are scored when the ball is thrown in the basket. You can't run with the ball. It is played with two teams.

_____
_____
_____
_____
_____

1 Decide si la frase muestra un superlativo o un comparativo. Escribe S o C.

  a Un ordenador es menos práctico que una tableta. _____

  b Mi teléfono es el más moderno. _____

  c Mi hermana quiere comprar un teléfono más moderno. _____

  d Tiene una pantalla mucho más grande. _____

  e Es uno de los aparatos más caros. _____

  f Es el mejor de todos. _____

2 Completa estas frases utilizando el comparativo.

  Ejemplo: *Mi hermano es muy inteligente.*

  Pues, mi hermana es más inteligente que tu hermano.

  a Mi hermano es muy trabajador.

  Mi hermana es _____ tu hermano.

  b Mi teléfono es uno de los mejores.

  Mi teléfono es aun _____ el tuyo.

  c Vivo en un piso muy moderno.

  Yo vivo en un piso _____.

3 Completa estas frases con un superlativo.

  Ejemplo: *Mi hermano es muy inteligente.*

  Pues, mi hermana es la más inteligente de la clase.

  a Voy a comprar un coche y es muy rápido.

  Mi coche es _____ del mundo.

  b Siempre llevo ropa cara.

  Mi ropa es _____.

  c Soy muy bueno hablando español.

  Soy _____ de la clase.

4 Analiza los datos que compara las diferencias entre las familias de hoy en día y las de hace 40 años. Escribe un párrafo comparando las diferencias, evita utilizar datos numéricos y utiliza los adjetivos que encontrarás a lado de esta actividad.

  Ejemplo: *El divorcio es mucho más común en España hoy que en los años setenta.*

	hace 40 años	hoy
número de bodas por mil habitantes por año	7	3
número de bodas religiosas por mil habitantes por año	7	1
edad típica de los hombres en el momento de casarse	25	37
edad típica de las mujeres en el momento de casarse	22	32
porcentaje de hijos de madre no casada	1	40
número medio de hijos en una familia	2.7	1.5
duración típica de matrimonio (años)	28	15
porcentaje de matrimonios entre personas del mismo sexo	0	2

Gramática

Comparatives are formed using the expressions *más … que* and *menos … que*. Remember to make the adjective agree.

*Mi hermano es **más** lento **que** una tortuga.*

*Una tortuga sería **menos** lenta **que** mi hermano.*

Superlatives are formed using the correct word for 'the' with *más* or *menos*.

*Mi hermano es **el más** lento.*

*La tortuga es uno de **los** animales **más** longevos.*

*Mi profesora es **la menos** organizada de todos.*

Gramática

Malo and bueno have irregular comparative/superlative forms:

peor – worse / ***el** peor* (the worst)

mejor – better / ***el** mejor* (the best)

*Mi hermanastra es **la** mejor para resolver problemas.* (My step-sister is the best at solving problems.)

Mayor and *menor* mean 'greater/older' and 'lesser/younger'.

un problema mayor es (a greater problem is)

Soy la menor. (I am the youngest.)

relevante	prevalente
popular	común
numeroso	típico
importante	regular
frecuente	joven
habitual	

Consejo

Only use *lo* if you mean 'the thing'. Do not automatically use it for superlatives.

el mejor / la mejor – the best
el más rápido – the quickest

lo mejor – the best thing
lo más rápido – the quickest thing

1 Lee las palabras de abajo y decide si forman parte de tu perfil o de tu estado.

| estudiante | cansado/a | en el instituto | español/a |
| joven | inteligente | alto/a | preocupado/a |

Perfil (ser)	Estado (estar)

> **Gramática**
>
> Spanish has two verbs 'to be'.
>
> *Ser* is for things that would go in your profile.
>
> *Estar* is for things that would go in your status.
>
> See the verb tables starting on page 84 for the conjugation of the verbs *ser* and *estar* in different tenses.

2 Lee las frases y en cada caso, explica la razón por la cual se utiliza *ser/estar*. Usa una hoja de papel aparte para escribir las razones.

a Voy a ser profesor.

b Mi profesor está enfermo.

c Mi sueño es ir a vivir en España.

d Madrid es la capital de España.

e Madrid está en España.

f Estoy comiendo.

> **Gramática**
>
> *Ser* is used for:
>
> profession, nationality, physical qualities, age, permanent qualities, definitions and identity
>
> *Estar* is used for:
>
> position, temporary state, verbs in the present continuous

3 Escoge el verbo correcto.

a **Ser / Estar** mujer no es fácil.

b Las mujeres **somos / estamos** cansadas de injusticias.

c Los manifestantes **son / están** en la cárcel.

d Él **es / está** mi esposo.

4 Traduce las frases al español.

a My parents are socialists. _____

b My friends are in Spain. _____

c You are very clever but a bit tired and bored. _____
_____

d Normally he is very quiet but today he is nervous so he is talking too much.
_____
_____

> **Gramática**
>
> Some words change their meaning depending on whether *ser* or *estar* is used.
>
> *Estoy aburrida* – I am bored
> *Es aburrido* – It is boring
>
> *Estoy incómodo* – I am uncomfortable
> *La silla es incómoda* – The chair is uncomfortable
>
> *Estoy muy nervioso* – I am very nervous (now)
> *Soy muy nervioso* – I am a very nervous person
>
> *Está muy callada* – She's very quiet (now)
> *Es muy callada* – She's a very quiet person
>
> *¿Estás listo?* – Are you ready?
> *¿Eres listo?* – Are you clever?
>
> *Está molesto* – He's annoyed
> *Es muy molesto* – It's very annoying

> **Consejo**
>
> Be careful with sentences like this: I am old and fed up. – *Soy viejo y estoy enfadado.*
>
> Also remember sometimes Spanish will not use 'to be': *tengo diecisiete años*; *hace mucho frío.*

1 Traduce las frases al español.

a It has changed. _____

b They have progressed. _____

c I have decided. _____

d It has decreased. _____

e You (plural) have finished. _____

f We have invented. _____

g You (singular) have changed. _____

h They have finished. _____

i They have decided. _____

j We have progressed. _____

2 Cambia el verbo del pretérito al perfecto.

Ejemplo: El partido comenzó. *El partido ha comenzado.*

a Hernández marcó un gol. _____

b Hernández y Albero discutieron. _____

c El árbitro expulsó a los dos jugadores. _____

d El Barcelona perdió. _____

e Ganamos el partido. _____

3 Subraya y luego traduce los verbos en el perfecto.

En los últimos años hemos experimentado una transformación en el mundo del fútbol. Se ha convertido en un deporte tanto para chicas como para chicos. Los institutos han cambiado la organización de las clases de educación física para adaptarse a una nueva realidad que han tenido que reconocer que existe.

_____

_____

_____

_____

4 Utiliza los verbos que has identificado en la actividad 3 para escribir un párrafo sobre los cambios en otro tema que has estudiado como, por ejemplo, la familia o la tecnología.

_____

_____

_____

_____

_____

_____

_____

_____

⚙ Gramática

The perfect tense is used to say what *has happened*. It is formed with the present tense of the auxiliary verb *haber* ('to have') plus the past participle ('happened/eaten/broken').

he hablado (I have spoken)

ha comido (he has eaten)

The present tense of *haber*:

| he | has | ha |
| hemos | habéis | han |

The past participle of regular *-ar* verbs ends in *-ado*: *hablado, jugado, nadado*.

For regular *-er* and *-ir* verbs it ends in *-ido*: *comido, venido, salido*.

1 Empareja los participios con el infinitivo.

hacer	poner	abrir
romper	decir	volver
cubrir	morir	ver

a visto _____

b hecho _____

c roto _____

d cubierto _____

e puesto _____

f dicho _____

g muerto _____

h abierto _____

i vuelto _____

> **Gramática**
>
> Some verbs have irregular past participles.
>
> *escribir → escrito* (written)
>
> *romper → roto* (broken)
>
> Where a verb has an irregular past participle, the verb *haber* is used as normal to make the perfect tense. See page 23.

2 Escribe lo que significan en inglés las palabras a–i.

3 Traduce al español.

a I have seen. _____

b We have broken. _____

c He has written. _____

d They have discovered. _____

e She has returned. _____

f It has died. _____

g You (singular) have seen. _____

h They have said. _____

4 Completa este texto con la forma correcta de los verbos. Memoriza la historia para recordar los participios irregulares.

El detective ha ª _____ que ha

ᵇ _____ a la escena del crimen donde el padre ha

ᶜ _____ que su hijo ha ᵈ _____ la

ventana que su esposa ha ᵉ _____ cuando la sirvienta lo

ha ᶠ _____ aunque el hijo ha ᵍ _____

que no lo ha ʰ _____. Lo bueno es que nadie ha

ⁱ _____.

a escribir	**f** ver
b volver	**g** decir
c descubrir	**h** hacer
d romper	**i** morir
e abrir	

1 Subraya los tres verbos en el condicional perfecto. Identifica con un círculo los tres verbos en el futuro perfecto.

habrá terminado   habremos decidido   habrían cambiado

han llegado   habríamos salido   habré ido

ha comenzado   habría jugado

2 Traduce al inglés los verbos que has identificado en la actividad 1.

_____   _____

_____   _____

_____   _____

3 Escribe la forma correcta del verbo en el futuro perfecto.

a Yo _____ antes de las dos. (*comer*)

b Nosotros _____ ya. (*salir*)

c Mis padres _____ antes. (*llegar*)

4 Escribe la forma correcta del verbo en el condicional perfecto.

a Miguel _____ antes de llegar. (*comer*)

b Violeta _____ no venir. (*decidir*)

c Tú _____ el plan. (*cambiar*)

5 Traduce al inglés.

Dentro de diez años habremos descubierto nuevas drogas que habrán impedido el crecimiento del pelo. Me imagino que los peluqueros habrían protestado, pero que nadie les habría escuchado, ya que se habrán vuelto innecesarios. De hecho, creo que habríamos enviado a los peluqueros a colonizar otro planeta.

_____

_____

_____

_____

_____

_____

6 Ahora tapa el texto original e intenta traducir tu versión inglesa al español.

_____

_____

_____

_____

_____

_____

_____

🄵 Gramática

The future perfect is formed using the future tense of the auxiliary verb *haber* plus past participle.

habré hablado (I will have spoken)

habrán comido (they will have eaten)

The future tense of the verb *haber* is:

habré	habrás	habrá
habremos	habréis	habrán

The conditional perfect is formed using the conditional tense of *haber* plus past participle.

habría hablado (I would have spoken)

habrías comido (you would have eaten)

The conditional tense of the verb *haber* is:

habría	habrías	habría
habríamos	habríais	habrían

For the formation of the past participle see page 23.

1 Subraya los cuatro verbos en el pluscuamperfecto.

habíamos ido

_____

habéis cambiado

_____

habrían decidido

_____

habíais tenido

_____

habían sido

_____

te habías enamorado

_____

> **⚑ Gramática**
>
> The pluperfect tense is formed with the imperfect tense of the auxiliary verb *haber* plus the past participle.
>
> *había hablado* (I had spoken)
>
> *habíamos comido* (we had eaten)
>
> The imperfect tense of *haber* is:
>
> | | | |
> |---|---|---|
> | *había* | *habías* | *había* |
> | *habíamos* | *habíais* | *habían* |
>
> For the formation of the past participle see page 23.

2 Traduce al inglés los verbos que has identificado en la actividad 1.

3 Cambia estos verbos al pluscuamperfecto.

a Su novio <u>ha cometido</u> un crimen.

_____

b <u>Hemos sido</u> testigos del crimen.

_____

c <u>He visto</u> toda la serie.

_____

4 Pon estos verbos en el pluscuamperfecto.

a Nosotros _____ al aeropuerto. (*llegar*)

b El vuelo _____ muy tarde. (*llegar*)

c El avión _____ una avería. (*tener*)

d El piloto _____ de no preocuparse. (*decir*)

e Yo _____ ir a Tenerife. (*decidir*)

5 Lee la historia completa de la telenovela *Al Filo de la Muerte*. Los verbos están en el presente. Cambia los verbos al pluscuamperfecto para introducir el último episodio, narrando la historia al revés. 'Previamente...'

Tracy López <u>tiene</u> un novio en Los Ángeles. <u>Es</u> testigo de un crimen que su novio comete. La policía le <u>da</u> una nueva identidad. Se <u>va</u> a vivir a México. Trabaja en un hospital donde <u>conoce</u> a un doctor prestigioso. La familia del doctor <u>ha muerto</u> en el terremoto de 1986. <u>Se enamora</u> del doctor. Su ex novio <u>escapa</u> de la cárcel. Viene a México a buscarla.

Ejemplo: Previamente... *su ex novio había venido a México a buscarla.*

Previamente su ex novio... _____

Previamente Tracy... _____

Previamente la familia del doctor... _____

Previamente Tracy... _____

Previamente Tracy... _____

Previamente la policía... _____

Previamente Tracy... _____

Previamente Tracy... _____

1 Empareja el tiempo verbal correcto (a–c) con las frases (i–vi). Luego tradúcelas al inglés.

a Pluscuamperfecto   **b** Futuro perfecto   **c** Condicional perfecto

i Su primo había nacido un par de años antes. _____

_____

ii La inmigración habrá dejado de ser un problema. _____

_____

iii Los integrantes del grupo se habían conocido en Los Ángeles. _____

_____

iv Ya te habrían dicho si te necesitaban. _____

_____

v No habrá habido cambios innecesarios. _____

_____

vi ¿Quién habría podido ser el más importante? _____

_____

2a Cambia estos verbos a la forma continua.

Ejemplo: *jugamos – estamos jugando*

a pienso _____   **d** hablaban _____

b cambian _____   **e** corríamos _____

c apoyas _____

2b Cambia estos verbos a la forma sencilla.

Ejemplo: *estábamos jugando – jugábamos*

a estoy intentando _____   **d** estaba pensando _____

b estaban esperando _____   **e** estáis trabajando _____

c está lloviendo _____

3 Subraya los seis verbos con cambio de raíz. En cada caso escribe el infinitivo del verbo.

La situación en la zona afectada por las inundaciones requiere ayuda inmediata. Puede haber miles de heridos y nuestro reportero nos dice que hay animales atrapados que mueren de frío y de hambre. Los miembros del público que quieren contribuir juegan un papel importante.

1 _____

2 _____

3 _____

4 _____

5 _____

6 _____

4 Traduce al inglés. Fíjate en las frases con *se*.

El flamenco se asocia con la región de Andalucía. Se practica en fiestas y también se ve en bares para los turistas. Se piensa que es un tipo de baile, pero en realidad se trata de un canto que se acompaña con música de guitarra.

_____

_____

_____

_____

5 Completa la traducción utilizando *se*.

✅ **Consejo**

Remember, Spanish avoids the passive voice by using *se*.

Se habla español. (Spanish is spoken.)

a For many Spanish people, the summer is spent in their village.

Para muchos españoles, el verano _____ en su pueblo. (*pasar*)

b The heat of the city is avoided.

El calor de la ciudad _____ . (*evitar*)

c Cultural events are organised.

_____ eventos culturales. (*organizar*)

d Friendships are maintained.

Las amistades _____ . (*mantener*)

e Parties are celebrated in social clubs which are called *peñas*.

_____ fiestas en clubs que _____ peñas. (*celebrar, llamar*)

6 Completa escogiendo el tiempo verbal adecuado.

✅ **Consejo**

One of these verbs needs the 'strong' form of the preterite.

Ejemplo: Hace un año mi hermano *fue* a vivir a los Estados Unidos. (*ir*)

a La semana que viene nosotros _____ a España. (*ir*)

b En la Navidad del año pasado los Reyes Magos me

_____ muchos regalos. (*traer*)

c Cada año mi hermana _____ a visitarnos. (*venir*)

d Este último año _____ muy difícil. (*ser*)

e Actualmente _____ español. (*estudiar*)

f Mi hermana _____ su partido ayer. (*ganar*)

g Yo _____ los deberes de mi amigo cuando entró mi profesor. (*copiar*)

✅ **Consejo**

You have seen these tenses on individual pages in this section. Can you pick the right one in each case?

7 Categoriza estos verbos. Escribe en una hoja de papel aparte lo que significan en inglés.

presente	pretérito	imperfecto	futuro	participio pasado

presente	pretérito	imperfecto	futuro	participio pasado
digo	juego	comió	quiso	hago
dicho	jugaba	comido	quiere	hizo
dije	jugaré	como	queríamos	hacían
decía	jugué	comía	querido	hecho
diré	jugado	comeremos	querrán	hará

8 Traduce los verbos al inglés. Explica en inglés la formación gramátical del verbo.

Ejemplo:
prefiero *I prefer, present tense radical changing, 1st person of preferir*

a tengo _____ _____

b saldrán _____ _____

c estuvimos _____ _____

d corría _____ _____

e ha hablado _____ _____

f iríamos _____

g había vuelto _____ _____

h aprendemos _____ _____

i volvieron _____ _____

j entendimos _____ _____

> **✓ Consejo**
> Once you've filled in the grammatical form, check that you translated the word accurately in the first place.

9 Escribe en español.

a we like _____

b they think _____

c she has finished _____

d you went _____

e I have been _____

f there is _____

g I am reading _____

h we stayed _____

i they arrived _____

j we said _____

k they got dressed _____

> **✓ Consejo**
> It might help to make a note first, reminding yourself what person and what tense you need. For example, for the first sentence: 1st person plural, present tense.

10 Cambia estas frases según se indica.

a ¿Has terminado tus deberes? (→ *usted*) _____

b Mi hermano llega el martes. (→ *pretérito*) _____

c Me duele la cabeza. (→ *nosotros*) _____

d Te ves muy guapo. (→ *vosotros*) _____

e Me fui a Madrid. (→ *futuro, ella*) _____

f Quiero dormir. (→ *nosotros*) _____

g Mi primo ha venido. (→ *pluscuamperfecto*) _____

h Vive en Alicante. (→ *imperfecto*) _____

11 Escoge el verbo correcto.

a   Mis padres **son** / **están** en Guanajuato.

b   Guanajuato **es** / **está** en México.

c   Mi tía **es** / **está** muy joven.

d   Quiero **ser** / **estar** astronauta.

e   Mi profesor **es** / **está** trabajando.

f   Las cosas **son** / **están** cambiando.

g   **Soy** / **Estoy** enferma y no puedo estudiar.

h   Mi padre **es** / **está** enfermero.

> ☑ **Consejo**
>
> With numbers, use *más de / menos de* instead of *que*.
>
> *Invitamos a más de cien personas*
>
> With a negative expression, *más que* can mean 'only'.
>
> *No tengo más que tres euros.* (I only have three euros.)

12 Traduce al inglés.

a   Mi hermana menor juega mejor que yo. _____

_____

b   Mi hermano mayor marcó más de cinco goles. _____

_____

c   Yo no marqué tantos goles como él. _____

_____

d   La que más goles marcó fue mi hermana. _____

_____

e   Tanto mi hermano como mi hermana son muy buenos. _____

_____

f   Soy el peor de la familia. _____

g   Quien trabaja más soy yo. _____

h   Mi hermana no estudia tanto como mi hermano. _____

_____

i   Mis hermanos no son tan trabajadores como yo. _____

_____

j   Cuanto más trabajo, más aprendo. _____

> ☑ **Consejo**
>
> *tanto … como …* (as … as …) can often be translated as 'both … and …'.

13 Traduce el texto al español.

Rugby is considered quite dangerous but my little brother is very good. He plays very well and is the best in his year. He used to train at the weekend but now he only plays at school. He has played for the school and they won all their matches. He would play for a club but he has to go to my dad's at the weekends. He is going to play for Scotland one day.

_____

_____

_____

_____

_____

_____

1 Traduce estas frases al inglés, poniendo atención al masculino/femenino.

a Es mi artista favorito. _____

b Es una modelo. _____

c Es actor. _____

d Es bailarín. _____

e Es compositora. _____

f Es diseñador de moda. _____

g Es una autora muy conocida. _____

h Es una celebridad y es muy famoso. _____

i El artista inglés es una estrella del rock. Vive en España. _____

> ✅ **Consejo**
>
> Look closely at all the information in the sentence, to decide if you need to put 'he…' or 'she…'.

2 Traduce los verbos subrayados al inglés.

a <u>Ha sido</u> difícil decidir. _____

b <u>Está trabajando</u> en España. _____

c <u>Nos gusta</u> mucho su trabajo. _____

d <u>Traje</u> un pastel para la fiesta. _____

e <u>Tiene</u> tiempo para mejorar. _____

f <u>Terminará</u> pronto. _____

g <u>Trabajaba</u> sola. _____

h <u>Sería</u> mejor comenzar de nuevo. _____

> ✅ **Consejo**
>
> Accurate identification of tenses is key to successful translation.

3 Traduce estas frases al inglés.

a Es uno de los mejores cantantes españoles.

_____

b Es el edificio más conocido de la ciudad.

_____

c Tiene un hermano menos famoso.

_____

d Sería mejor pasar el día entero allí.

_____

e No había visitado una ciudad tan bonita.

_____

4 Da una traducción mejor.

a Se ha hecho muy famoso. *It has made itself very famous.*

_____

b Se comenzó en 1896. *It started itself in 1896.*

_____

c Se considera una obra maestra. *It considers itself a masterpiece.*

_____

d Se puede visitar. *It can visit itself.*

_____

e Se recomienda pasar varias horas allí. *It recommends itself to spend several hours there.*

_____

5 Traduce al inglés.

Fergie es una de muchas celebridades con raíces mexicanas. Ha sido bailarina, compositora, modelo y diseñadora de moda pero es más conocida como actriz y cantante. Ha colaborado con algunos de los mejores artistas del rap. Hoy en día está desarrollando una carrera de artista en solitario. Menos conocido es su trabajo para asociaciones benéficas, y el hecho de que su marca de perfume ha sido una de las que ha tenido más éxito.

✅ **Consejo**

Watch out for the differences between Spanish and English with articles:
soy estudiante (I am **a** student)
And word order:
director de cine (film director)

_____

_____

_____

_____

_____

_____

_____

_____

6 Traduce al inglés.

Hoy, los teléfonos inteligentes nos permiten participar en las redes sociales mientras se prepara la cena o durante una reunión de trabajo. Trajeron enormes beneficios para la vida social y laboral pero también tienen su lado negativo. La tecnología modificó nuestros hábitos, y para algunos se ha convertido en una obsesión. Se ha calculado que típicamente se consulta el móvil hasta ciento cincuenta veces al día.

✅ **Consejo**

Identify exactly what verb tense is being used in each case.

_____

_____

_____

_____

_____

_____

_____

7 Traduce al inglés.

Se calcula que la Basílica de la Sagrada Familia se completará en el año 2026. Serán ciento cuarenta y cuatro años desde que comenzó su construcción. Es la obra maestra del arquitecto catalán Gaudí, y la atracción más famosa de la ciudad de Barcelona. Durante los primeros dieciséis años de su construcción, Gaudí vivía en la catedral, y hoy está enterrado en la cripta. Su diseño incorpora el estilo orgánico de su autor al simbolismo de la Iglesia Católica. En el plano original había dieciocho agujas, incluyendo una de ciento setenta y dos metros que sería la aguja de iglesia más alta del mundo.

✅ **Consejo**

Read the whole text first. Some words, including unfamiliar technical terms, can be deduced from the context.

_____

_____

_____

_____

_____

_____

1 Empareja las traducciones.

a	She checked the results.		**i**	Revisó mis documentos.
b	He checked his pocket.		**ii**	Comprobó los resultados.
c	He checked her story.		**iii**	Buscó en su bolsillo.
d	She checked my documents.		**iv**	Comparó su agenda con la mía.
e	He checked his diary against mine.		**v**	Verificó su historia.
f	She checked the expenses.		**vi**	Monitorizó los gastos.
g	He checked his temperature.		**vii**	Le tomó la temperatura.
h	She checked with her team.		**viii**	Controla la calidad.
i	He checks the quality.		**ix**	Consultó con su equipo.

2 Utiliza los ejemplos de la actividad 1 para completar la traducción. Hay varias posibilidades en cada caso.

✓ Consejo

The activities on this page focus on words where there are several possible translations of an English word. Sometimes there are slight variations in meaning or there may be different possible translations which are all correct.

a *She checked the garage.* _____ el garaje.

b *He checked the score.* _____ el marcador.

c *He checked his pulse.* _____ su pulso.

d *She checked his performance.* _____ su rendimiento.

e *We checked the weather forecast.* _____ el pronóstico meteorológico.

f *She checked her watch.* _____ su reloj.

3 Escoge la mejor opción para completar la traducción.

a *It was an act of charity.* Fue un acto de _____.

b *He worked for a charity.* Trabajaba para _____.

c *He has done charity work.* Ha hecho labores _____.

d *She did charity work.* Trabajó _____.

e *My boss isn't known for his charity.* A mi jefe no se le conoce por su _____.

f *We've updated the kitchen.* Hemos _____ la cocina.

g *I get frequent updates about my family.* Recibo _____ frecuentes de mi familia.

h *My computer is being updated.* Mi ordenador se está _____.

i *The book has an updates section.* El libro tiene una sección de _____.

j *We have to update our procedures.* Tenemos que _____ nuestros procedimientos.

i	de voluntario	**v**	noticias
ii	caritativas	**vi**	revisiones
iii	caridad	**vii**	actualizando
iv	una organización benéfica	**viii**	actualizar
		ix	renovado

4 Traduce al español.

Taboo is another rock star with Mexican roots. His real name is Jaime Luis Gomez. He is American but his father was born in Morelia, the most beautiful city in Mexico. He is a singer and actor, best known as a member of the Black Eyed Peas. He has sung in Spanish and English. As a solo artist he has recorded a song to support a cancer charity.

_____

_____

_____

_____

_____

✓ Consejo

The texts and exercises on pages 31–32 will give you some support with vocabulary and structures, but make sure you adapt them carefully to translate accurately.

✓ Consejo

Use the text on page 32 to remind you when Spanish does or doesn't need to use the indefinite article 'a' when talking about jobs.

✓ Consejo

You may need up to eight words to translate the two words, 'cancer charity'.

5 Traduce al español.

The smart watch is changing our lifestyle. Instead of checking your phone, your watch can check on you. It registers your activity and alerts you to events. They are sold with the promise that they bring health benefits, but for many people they have become an irritation, with constant reminders and updates. And now you can buy a toothbrush which communicates with your phone, which is connected to your watch, which tells you to brush your teeth more often.

_____

_____

_____

_____

_____

_____

✓ Consejo

Remember Spanish uses *se* to avoid the passive voice.

6 Traduce al español.

Córdoba Cathedral is recognised as a masterpiece of the architecture of *Al-Andalus*. It is the most important monument in Córdoba and one of the most visited sites in Spain. It was originally built as a mosque. It was the second biggest mosque in the world at the time. The Catholic cathedral was built in the middle of the mosque. The architect was Hernán Ruiz. When the Emperor Charles the Fifth saw the building, he said, 'You have destroyed what was unique in the world and you have put in its place what can be seen everywhere.'

_____

_____

_____

_____

_____

_____

✓ Consejo

Use the *vosotros* form to translate the Emperor's quote.

1 Isidoro, Raquel, Borja y Nerea tienen información sobre unos objetos que han desaparecido. Son: i unos pasteles, ii un reloj, iii una foto, iv unas llaves. ¿De qué cosa (i–iv) están hablando?

a Isidoro: Mi madre la miraba. _____

b Raquel: Mi hermano los comió. _____

c Borja: Nadie las ha visto. _____

d Nerea: Mi padre lo llevó. _____

2 Empareja las frases (a–d) con los objetos (i–iv).

a Lo comí.

b Las comeré.

c No los he comido.

d La quiero comer.

i un helado

ii dos huevos

iii una ensalada

iv unas aceitunas

3 Reemplaza el objeto de estas frases con el pronombre.

Ejemplo: Reemplaza el objeto. *Reemplázalo.*

a Los jóvenes toman la educación muy en serio. _____

b Valoramos nuestros derechos. _____

c Tenemos que aceptar nuestras responsabilidades. _____

d Estaba explorando varias posibilidades. _____

e He dejado mi trabajo. _____

4 Utiliza pronombres para evitar repetición. Indica cuáles son las palabras a reemplazar. Pon el pronombre correcto en el lugar adecuado.

Me interesan mucho las figuras coleccionables de ciencia ficción. Cuando voy a las tiendas siempre busco figuras coleccionables de ciencia ficción. Por ejemplo el fin de semana estaba con mis amigos y vi una figura que necesitaba para mi colección. Compré la figura que necesitaba para mi colección pero era muy cara. Mi colección tiene un valor muy elevado pero no voy a vender mi colección de figuras coleccionables de ciencia ficción. Voy a seguir coleccionando figuras de ciencia ficción.

🗲 Gramática

Direct object pronouns are:

me	me
te	you
lo / la	him / her / it
nos	us
os	you
los / las	them

Pronouns go in front of a conjugated verb or on the end of an infinitive.

Lo comí.

Voy a comerlo.

Lo voy a comer.

In perfect tenses, the conjugated verb is the auxiliary verb *haber*.

Lo he comido.

Las habíamos comido.

Siento mucho haberlo comido.

With imperatives and present participles, pronouns go on the end. An accent may be needed to keep the stress in the correct place.

Cómelo. (Eat it.)

Estaba comiéndolo. (I was eating it.)

1 **Completa con el pronombre correcto.**

a *He sent a message to her.*

_____ envió un mensaje.

b *He wrote a letter to us.*

_____ escribió una carta.

c *I give a hug to you (singular).*

_____ doy un abrazo.

d *I am going to offer two options to you (plural).*

Voy a ofrecer _____ dos opciones.

2 **Traduce al inglés. Utiliza la palabra 'to' o 'for'.**

a No le dije nada. _____

b Nos mostró las fotos. _____

c Te voy a regalar una bici. _____

d Les explicó la gramática. _____

e No me importa. _____

f Me reparó el aparato. _____

3 **Escribe estas frases en inglés utilizando la palabra 'to' o 'for'. Luego tradúcelas al español.**

a He told me a secret.

_____

_____

b They sent her an email.

_____

_____

c I will give him a present.

_____

_____

d She wrote him a poem.

_____

_____

e They are offering me a special price.

_____

_____

f They sold him the computer.

_____

_____

g They bought us a car.

_____

_____

Gramática

Indirect object pronouns are:

me	to me
te	to you
le	to him / her / it
nos	to us
os	to you
les	to them

Pronouns go in front of a conjugated verb or on the end of an infinitive.

Me interesa.

No me va a interesar.

No va a interesarme.

With the perfect tense, the conjugated verb is the auxiliary verb *haber*.

Le he hablado. (I have spoken to him.)

Es importante haberle hablado. (It is important to have spoken to him.)

Pronouns go on the end of present participles and imperatives. An accent may be needed to keep the stress in the correct place.

Dame eso. (Give me that.)

Estoy hablándole. (I am talking to her.)

✓ Consejo

It is important to learn which verbs in Spanish take indirect objects, as English often omits the 'to'.

She showed him the evidence. = She showed the evidence to him. *Le mostró la evidencia.*

Sometimes the indirect object is better translated as 'for'.

Le escribió la receta. (He wrote down the recipe for her.)

1 Empareja el español con el inglés.

a	Fue dañado.	**i**	It has been fixed.
b	Ha sido reparado.	**ii**	It is going to be replaced.
c	Va a ser reemplazado.	**iii**	It is imported.
d	Puede haber sido inventado.	**iv**	It was damaged.
e	Es importado.	**v**	It might have been invented.

2 Empareja las dos mitades de las frases.

a	La tableta fue	**i**	reparado.
b	El ordenador	**ii**	fueron inventadas.
c	Los aparatos	**iii**	fue reparada.
d	El aparato fue	**iv**	reparada.
e	Las tabletas	**v**	fue vendido.
f	La tableta	**vi**	han sido reparados.

3 Escribe estas frases utilizando la voz pasiva.

a El ordenador se vendió a un precio excesivo.

_____

b Inventaron un nuevo tipo de ordenador.

_____

c Han reparado mi portátil.

_____

d Repararon la tableta.

_____

4 Lee y subraya las frases donde NO se podría evitar el uso de la voz pasiva utilizando *se* o la tercera persona.

El ordenador fue adoptado como una parte necesaria de cada casa. Fue utilizado todos los días para diferentes tareas. Luego la tableta fue inventada. La tableta es vendida en cantidades impresionantes. Además de ser utilizada en casa, es utilizada por gran cantidad de profesionales en su trabajo. Dentro de poco, el ordenador será reemplazado completamente por nuevos inventos.

5 Completa la traducción.

a New technologies have been developed.

Nuevas tecnologías _____.

b Most jobs will be carried out by robots.

La mayoría de los trabajos _____ por robots.

c I have been replaced by a computer.

_____ por un ordenador.

⌨ Gramática

The passive voice is formed with the verb *ser* plus the past participle.

The past participle needs to agree for gender and number.

El explorador fue comido por un monstruo. (The explorer was eaten by a monster.)

La ventana fue rota por un niño. (The window was broken by a child.)

Los exámenes han sido aplazados. (The exams have been postponed.)

Spanish often avoids the passive voice by using *se* or by using a third person construction: *tiraron muchas flores* (many flowers were thrown). The advantage of using the passive voice is you can use *por* to say who the action was performed by.

See page 20 for how to avoid the passive voice by using *se*.

See pages 23 and 24 for the formation of the past participle.

✓ Consejo

You may see *estar* plus past participle: *La ventana estaba rota* (The window was broken). This is a description of a broken window. It is not the passive voice saying how the window was broken. The passive voice always uses *ser*.

✓ Consejo

Be very careful about gender and number, especially in 5b.

1. Lee las frases de abajo. En cada caso, escribe la razón (1–3, en el cuadro de gramática) por la cual se requiere el subjuntivo.

a   No creo que el español sea difícil. ___

b   Siento que tu perro esté muerto. ___

c   Mis padres no quieren que sea dentista. ___

d   Quiero que hagas tus deberes. ___

e   Es muy decepcionante que no hayas hecho tus deberes. ___

f   No es muy probable que Nathan haya hecho sus deberes. ___

g   Mi padre no piensa que estudiar sea importante. ___

h   Necesito que vayas a la tienda a comprar pan. ___

i   Es muy importante que vengas a mi fiesta. ___

j   Es chocante que no quiera venir a la fiesta conmigo. ___

2 Explica en inglés por qué se utiliza el subjuntivo o por qué no.

a   Quiero nadar en la piscina. _____

b   No quiero que nades en el mar. _____

c   No pienso que sea peligroso. _____

d   Pienso que es seguro. _____

e   Es muy emocionante que dos turistas hayan sido rescatados por el

helicóptero. _____

f   Dos turistas han sido rescatados. ¡Qué emocionante! _____

_____

3 Escribe el subjuntivo de estos verbos. Recuerda que todos aparecen en esta página.

you swim _____   you do _____

you come _____   you go _____

it is (ser) _____   they have (haber) _____

it is (estar) _____

4 Intenta identificar una regla que explique la formación del subjuntivo de los verbos en el presente. Explícalo en inglés.

Verbs that end in -**ar** _____
_____
_____
_____

Verbs that end in -**er** or -**ir** _____
_____
_____
_____
_____

Gramática

The subjunctive is a verb mood that can be found in present, perfect and imperfect tenses.

These are the three main categories for using the subjunctive:

1 Doubt/Improbability:

No pienso que, es poco probable que, no es verdad que, no hay nadie que

2 Value judgement/Emotion:

Lamento que …, es genial que …, me sorprende que …, es chocante que …

3 Wanting someone else to do something:

Mis padres quieren que…, los jóvenes insisten en que …, las autoridades determinan que …

---

1 ¿Cuál es el infinitivo de estos verbos?

a No creo que <u>puedas</u>. _____

b Quiero que me <u>ayudes</u>. _____

c Es importante que <u>entiendan</u>. _____

d Es imposible que <u>sepas</u>. _____

e Dudo que <u>llegue</u> a tiempo. _____

f Nadie piensa que <u>sea</u> posible. _____

g No creo que <u>venga</u>. _____

h Es insoportable que <u>digan</u> eso. _____

2 Indica cuáles están en el subjuntivo (S) y cuáles en el indicativo (I).

a Pienso que es muy divertido. ___

b Quiere que le ayude. ___

c No pienso que sea útil. ___

d Quiero ir al concierto. ___

e Es importante que me ayudes. ___

f Los jóvenes tienen muchas responsabilidades. ___

g No creo que tengamos muchos deberes. ___

★ 3 Cambia estos verbos al subjuntivo.

a nadamos _____

b corren _____

c hacen _____

d digo _____

e van _____

f jugamos _____

g sacan _____

★ 4 Completa estas frases con el verbo en el subjuntivo.

a No quiero que _____ tus pijamas. (*olvidar*)

b Es importante que Scott _____ buenas notas. (*sacar*)

c No creo que _____ posible. (*ser*)

d Necesito que tú me _____. (*explicar*)

e No les gusta que los adultos les _____ qué hacer. (*decir*)

f Mis padres quieren que mi hermano _____ a la universidad. (*ir*)

g No puedo impedir que mis amigos _____ tonterías. (*hacer*)

h Siento mucho que vosotros no _____ ganar. (*poder*)

Gramática

The subjunctive can be considered the opposite of the normal indicative mood, so the three verb classes take the opposite ending to normal. So -*ar* verbs have **e** endings and -*er*/-*ir* verbs have **a** endings.

nad**ar**:	nade	nades	nade
	nademos	nadéis	naden
com**er**:	coma	comas	coma
	comamos	comáis	coman
viv**ir**:	viva	vivas	viva
	vivamos	viváis	vivan

• Where a verb has an irregular first person form, this is the stem for the present subjunctive:

hacer → hago:

haga	hagas	haga
hagamos	hagáis	hagan

conocer → conozco:

conozca	conozcas	conozca
conozcamos	conozcáis	conozcan

• Radical changing verbs keep their stem change in the same persons in the subjunctive.

poder:

pueda	**pue**das	**pue**da
podamos	podáis	**pue**dan

• Verbs where the stem ends in *c, z, g* or *j* may need a spelling change to match the pronunciation.

sacar: sa**que**	jugar: jue**gu**e
tropezar: tropie**ce**	coger: co**j**a

• Irregular verbs can have irregular stems:

ir: **v**aya	haber: haya
saber: sepa	

1 Pon una tilde al lado de las frases que contienen un verbo en el subjuntivo. En cada caso explica por qué se requiere (o no) el subjuntivo.

Ejemplo:

No pienso que hayas terminado de comer absolutamente todas tus verduras. ☑

Requiere el subjuntivo porque está la expresión 'no pienso que'.

a Pienso que has escondido unas zanahorias debajo de tu tenedor. ☐

_____

b Quiero que hayas comido todo antes de encender el televisor. ☐

_____

c Has comido todo. ¡Qué bien! ☐

_____

d Qué bien que hayas comido todo. ☐

_____

e Pienso que has sido un muy buen niño. ☐

_____

f Me alegra que te hayas comportado bien. ☐

_____

> ### ☐ Gramática
>
> The perfect tense in the subjunctive mood is formed with the present subjunctive of the auxiliary verb *haber* plus the past participle.
>
> *No creo que <u>hayas ganado</u>.* (I don't think you've won.)
>
> The present subjunctive of *haber* is:
>
> | | | |
> |---|---|---|
> | *haya* | *hayas* | *haya* |
> | *hayamos* | *hayáis* | *hayan* |
>
> See pages 23 and 24 for the formation of the past participle.
>
> See page 38 for when to use the subjunctive.

★ 2 Cambia estas frases para expresar lo contrario. *No pienso que…* Necesitarás utilizar el subjuntivo.

a Pienso que los móviles han cambiado la vida.

_____

b Es verdad que la familia tradicional ha desaparecido.

_____

c Es mi opinión que la iglesia se ha adaptado a la vida moderna.

_____

d Sé que los españoles han cambiado su actitud hacia la monarquía.

_____

e Digo que ha sido muy importante preservar las costumbres regionales.

_____

f Supongo que has leído *La Sombra del Viento*.

_____

★ 3 Completa las frases utilizando el subjuntivo.

Es interesante que _____

_____

No creo que _____

_____

El gobierno insistió en que _____

_____

No es el caso que _____

_____

⬆ Gramática

Demonstrative adjectives are words like 'this', 'that', 'these' or 'those'.

Spanish has three different words for 'this/that':

este bolígrafo = this pen (near me)

ese bolígrafo = that pen (near you)

aquel bolígrafo = that pen (not near me or you)

Each one agrees for gender and number:

este	*esta*	*estos*	*estas*
ese	*esa*	*esos*	*esas*
aquel	*aquella*	*aquellos*	*aquellas*

Don't worry too much about picking the 'right' one out of *ese/este*. Concentrate on getting the correct form for gender and number. Notice the masculine singular forms do not end in *o*.

✅ Consejo

There is a neutral demonstrative pronoun *esto/eso/aquello* which is used to refer to a whole concept rather than a specific word:

Eso es perfecto.

Do not use it instead of the correct form when referring to a specific masculine or feminine noun.

---

1 Completa las frases con la forma correcta.

a _____ patatas están demasiado calientes. No las puedo comer. (*este*)

b _____ señor que vive en la casa de enfrente es un metiche. (*ese*)

c _____ políticos de Madrid no saben lo que hacen. (*aquel*)

d _____ dedo me duele. (*este*)

e _____ son mis gafas. Dámelas, por favor. (*ese*)

f _____ pantalones no son tuyos. Vete a cambiarlos. (*ese*)

✅ Consejo

You may see texts where an accent is used to distinguish the adjective from the pronoun.

Adjective: *este bolígrafo* (this pen)

Pronoun: *éste* (this one)

The Spanish Royal Academy has now said that the accent is no longer required.

---

2 Escoge la palabra correcta.

a **Eso** / **Ese** perro es mi favorito.

b Tengo dos gatos. **Eso** / **Ese** es el más cariñoso.

c Cuido de las mascotas de un vecino. **Eso** / **Ese** es mi negocio.

d Tengo un gato y una tortuga. **Esta** / **Aquella** es muy lenta.

e No quieren aceptar **este** / **esto** argumento.

f Tenemos que tirar **aquel** / **aquello** porque estorba.

✅ Consejo

In written Spanish you can see *este* and *aquel* (in the correct form) used to mean 'the latter' and 'the former'.

He vivido en Barcelona y en Sevilla: me gustan las dos ciudades pero esta es muy tradicional y aquella muy moderna.

---

3 Traduce al inglés.

Hay varios tipos de mascota y eso puede presentar un problema si quieres trabajar con animales. Este tipo de trabajo requiere conocimientos y experiencia. Esta es quizás lo más importante. Por ejemplo, entre esta tortuga y esa serpiente hay una gran diferencia, pero también este perro puede tener un carácter totalmente diferente a ese otro. Eso es lo que hace interesante el trabajo.

_____

_____

_____

_____

_____

_____

4 Ahora tapa el texto original e intenta traducir tu versión inglesa al español.

_____

_____

_____

_____

_____

_____

◳ Gramática

The Spanish possessive adjectives are:

mi /mis	my
tu / tus	your (sing)
su / sus	his / her / its
	your (*usted*)
nuestro / nuestra / nuestros / nuestras	our
vuestro / vuestra / vuestros / vuestras	your (pl)
su / sus	their
	your (*ustedes*)

They all agree with the noun for number. *Nuestro* and *vuestro* agree for gender.

Do not be fooled into thinking that 'his' is *su* and 'their' must be *sus*. Adjectives agree with the noun they describe, not the person.

Su amigo (their friend)   *Sus amigos* (their friends)

---

1 Completa con la palabra correcta.

a Fue a visitar a _____ amigo de España. (*her*)

b Me gusta ir con _____ familia. (*my*)

c Van a viajar con _____ amigo irlandés. (*their*)

d _____ abuelos viven en Málaga. (*our*)

e Tienen que llevar _____ pasaportes. (*their*)

f Han limitado _____ oportunidades. (*our*)

2 ¿Quién es el dueño de qué? Haz corresponder las personas con los objetos.

a Iratxe: Es mía. ____

b Paula: Son los míos. ____

c Virginia: Eso no es mío, esa es tuya, pero esas son mías. ____

d Alberto: El mío es este. ____

i un sombrero   ii una camiseta   iii unos guantes   iv unas zapatillas

3 Traduce al español.

I like your idea but mine is the best one. I like yours but not as much as mine. Our work is always the best, and our ideas are fantastic, usually yours but this time my one.

_____

_____

_____

_____

◳ Gramática

Possessive pronouns replace the noun.

mío / mía / míos / mías	mine
tuyo / tuya / tuyos / tuyas	yours (sing)
suyo / suya / suyos / suyas	his / hers / its
	yours (*usted*)
nuestro / nuestra / nuestros / nuestras	ours
vuestro / vuestra / vuestros / vuestras	yours (pl)
suyo / suya / suyos / suyas	theirs
	yours (*ustedes*)

Es mío. (It is mine.) *¿Eso es tuyo?* (Is this yours?)

They are usually used with the correct form of the word 'the'.

Es el mío. (It is my one.)

La tuya es la verde. (Yours is the green one.)

No me gusta el tuyo. (I don't like yours / your one.)

★ *Cuyo* means 'whose'.

La señora cuyo hijo habla español (The lady whose son speaks Spanish)

✅ Consejo

Remember NEVER to use -'s for possessives in Spanish.

my dad's room = the room of my dad: *el dormitorio de mi padre*

1 **Completa las frases con la palabra indicada.**

a No me gusta _____ de esas camisetas. (*not one*)

b Nos encantan _____ esos zapatos. (*all*)

c _____ de esos le gustaría. (*any*)

d Tu camisa está sucia. Necesitas ponerte _____. (*another one*)

e ¿Tienes _____ producto para el pelo? (*some*)

f ¿Tienes de _____ marca? (*another*)

g Los llevo _____ día. (*every*)

h No me pongo _____ cosa. (*cualquiera*)

2 **Traduce al inglés.**

a Tiene algunas ideas buenas. _____

b No tiene ninguna buena idea. _____

c Algunas son buenas ideas. _____

d Algunos tienen buenas ideas. _____
_____

e Tiene varias ideas. _____

f Tiene otra idea. _____

g Propone cualquier idea. _____

h Explora cada posibilidad. _____

i Explora todas las posibilidades. _____
_____

j Todo es posible. _____

3 **Traduce al español.**

a He has several good ideas, but some are better than others. _____
_____

b He has few good ideas, but not all are bad. _____
_____

c He has some ideas, some good, others bad. _____
_____

d Some people have good ideas, some have bad ones. _____
_____

e Another possibility is to explore all your ideas… _____
_____

f …then you can eliminate some but not all. _____
_____

g The problem is when you have no ideas at all. _____
_____

h Sometimes any idea is a good one. _____
_____

Gramática

These words are known as indefinite adjectives.

alguno	some
ninguno	not one
cualquiera	any / whatever
todo	all
cada	each
otro	another
varios	several
pocos	few

These words shorten in front of a masculine singular noun:

alguno → algún problema
ninguno → ningún problema

Cualquiera shortens in front of a masculine or a feminine noun:

cualquier problema, cualquier persona

Todo agrees for number and gender, while *cada* is invariable:

todos los días / cada día

Otro means 'another' without the need for the word *un* or *una*.

otra cosa (another thing)
otro día (another day)

Be careful with:

pocos (few/not many)
unos pocos (a few)
poco (not very) (adverb)
un poco (a little)

These words can act as indefinite pronouns:

alguno, ninguno, cualquiera, otro, todo, varios, pocos

Voy a comer otro. (I'm going to eat another one.)

He probado varios. (I have tried several.)

Gramática

For regular -ar verbs the imperative has these endings:

hablar: *habla* (singular) / *hablad* (plural) = speak

comer: *come* (singular) / *comed* (plural) = eat

vivir: *vive* (singular) / *vivid* (plural) = live

Radical changing verbs keep the change in the imperative:

Juega bien con tu hermano. (Play nicely with your brother.)

Pronouns go on the end of the imperative and an accent may be needed to keep the stress in the correct place:

¡Háblame! (Speak to me!)   *¡Cómelo!* (Eat it!)

The reflexive pronoun *os* on the end of a plural imperative makes it lose the *d*, otherwise it would look like the past participle:

¡Sentaos! (Sit down!)   *¡Levantaos!* (Stand up!)

Some verbs have irregular singular imperative forms.

Venir → ven   *¡Ven aquí!* (Come here!)

Gramática

For negative imperatives use the subjunctive:

¡No cantes tan alto! (Don't sing so loudly!)

¡No comas eso! (Don't eat that!)

¡No hagas eso! (Don't do that!)

For the formal *usted* form use the subjunctive for imperatives:

¡Venga! (Come!)

¡Entren! (Come in!)

See page 39 for the formation of the subjunctive.

1 Empareja los imperativos irregulares con el infinitivo.

a di
b sal
c haz
d sé
e ve
f ten
g pon
h ven

i venir
ii poner
iii decir
iv tener
v ser
vi hacer
vii salir
viii ir

2 Empareja las frases que significan lo mismo.

a No os gritéis.
b No guardéis secretos.
c No sigas peleando al día siguiente.
d No utilicéis palabrotas.

i Hablad de forma educada.
ii Confía en tu pareja.
iii Empieza cada día sin rencor.
iv Habla sin alzar la voz.

3 Traduce al inglés.

a Dame eso. _____
b Haz los deberes. _____
c Callaos. _____
d No pongas eso allí. _____
e No lo creas. _____
f Sacad vuestros cuadernos. _____

4 Escribe el verbo en la forma correcta.

a _____ lo que has escrito. (*leer*)
b _____ vuestro trabajo. (*terminar*)
c _____ tus cosas en orden. (*poner*)
d No _____ basura. (*tirar, tú*)
e _____ con cuidado. (*conducir, usted*)

1 Identifica las cuatro frases que contienen un verbo en el subjuntivo y tradúcelas al inglés.

   a Quiero ir a España para mejorar mi español. ☐

   b No necesitas ir a la biblioteca. ☐

   c No piensa que sea necesario. ☐

   d Necesitamos que nos ayudes con los deberes. ☐

   e No estudies tanto. ☐

   f Cree que necesitas descansar. ☐

   g Es una lástima que saques malas notas. ☐

   1 _____

   2 _____

   3 _____

   4 _____

2 Completa las frases con la forma correcta del verbo en el subjuntivo.

   a Tu padre quiere que _____ ingeniero. (*ser, tú*)

   b No voy a impedir que _____ ballet. (*hacer, tú*)

   c ¡Qué bien que _____ ganado el concurso! (*haber, ella*)

   d Mi profesor piensa que es mejor que _____ otro idioma. (*estudiar, yo*)

   e No pienso que _____ fácil hablar alemán. (*ser*)

3 Escribe la frase completa. Necesitarás el subjuntivo en cada caso.

Ejemplo: Es una pena / han expulsado al jugador
Es una pena que hayan expulsado al jugador.

   a Él no piensa / ha cometido una falta

   _____

   b No creo / llora

   _____

   c Necesita / el entrenador le ayuda

   _____

   d No quiere / le dicen qué hacer

   _____

   e Siento / el jefe no quiere hablarme

   _____

4 Traduce al español.

   a My teacher thinks that it is best that we do our homework.

   _____

   b Elena doesn't think it is hard to learn English.

   _____

   c Your dad wants to stop you being lazy.

   _____

   d It's great you have learned to speak Spanish.

   _____

   e Don't think you can't be successful.

   _____

5 Escribe estas frases utilizando la voz pasiva.

Ejemplo: El vino se elabora en el Rioja. *El vino es elaborado en el Rioja.*

a Los coches se fabrican en Zaragoza.

_____

b El acero se extrae en Asturias.

_____

c Las naranjas se cultivan en Valencia.

_____

d El país se gobierna desde Madrid.

_____

e La independencia catalana se reivindica en Barcelona.

_____

f El queso se produce en La Mancha.

_____

g La cerveza se consume en Inglaterra.

_____

h Aragón se conoce por sus paisajes impresionantes.

_____

> ✅ **Consejo**
>
> The structures and vocabulary on this page will give you some help with the translations on page 52.

> ✅ **Consejo**
>
> With *ser* the past participle needs to agree for gender and number.

6 Lee y completa con la forma correcta: *este, esta, estos, estas, estos* o *esto*.

a Soy muy buen ingeniero, y _____ va a ser importante para mi carrera.

b Busco una nueva novia y _____ va a ser el amor de mi vida.

c _____ coche es muy contaminante.

d No me acuerdo de haber comprado _____ guantes.

e No quiero volver a ver a _____ individuos.

f Está prohibido, y _____ no va a cambiar.

g _____ son demasiado caras.

h Iba a traer unos, pero podemos utilizar _____.

7 Lee la frase en español. Traduce la segunda frase al español.

a Golpeó la piñata con un palo.

He hit it with a stick.

_____

b Llenaron la piñata de dulces.

They filled it with sweets.

_____

c Colgamos las piñatas en el patio.

We hung them in the courtyard.

_____

d Regalaron dulces a los vecinos.

They gave sweets to them.

_____

e Su hija mandó una tarjeta a sus amigas.

She sent a card to them.

_____

f Su hija mandó una tarjeta a sus amigas.

She sent it to her friends.

_____

g Los Reyes Magos trajeron regalos para los niños.

They brought them presents.

_____

h Los Reyes Magos trajeron regalos para los niños.

They brought them for the children.

_____

8 Pon el verbo en el imperativo.

a beber (*tú*) _____

b correr (*tú, negativo*) _____

c dormir (*vosotros*) _____

d pensar (*tú*) _____

e ayudar (*usted*) _____

f venir (*ustedes*) _____

g beber (*tú, negativo*) _____

h ayudar (*vosotros, negativo*) _____

i decir (*usted, negativo*) _____

j poner (*tú*) _____

9 Cambia la forma de estos imperativos según se indica.

a ¡Levántate! (→ *vosotros*) _____

b ¡Come! (→ *negativo*) _____

c ¡Ven! (→ *usted*) _____

d ¡Vivid! (→ *tú*) _____

e ¡Dámelo! (→ *vosotros*) _____

f ¡Dámelo! (→ *usted*) _____

g ¡Dámelo! (→ *negativo*) _____

10 Empareja el español con el inglés.

a Dile que no vaya.

b No le digas que vaya.

c Permitidles que se queden.

d Oblíguelo a que se quede.

e Le obliga a irse.

f No le gusta que le digas.

g Haz que se vayan.

h Que se quede.

i Don't tell him to go.

ii Let them stay.

iii Tell him not to go.

iv Make him stay.

v She doesn't like you telling her.

vi Make them go.

vii She makes him go.

viii Let her stay.

11 Completa con la forma correcta de la palabra indicada.

a En la Edad Media los guerreros apoyaron a _____ rey. (*their*)

b Hoy elegimos a _____ presidentes. (*our*)

c _____ instituciones están corruptas. (*our*)

d _____ votos cuentan. (*your, plural*)

e Tenemos algunas instituciones _____ raíces están en la Edad Media. (*whose*)

f Sus costumbres eran menos civilizadas que _____ _____. (*ours*)

12 **Selecciona la palabra adecuada para completar cada frase.**

a _____ vez que te vas me pongo a llorar.

b _____ veces siento que no me quieres.

c _____ persona puede ver que te quiero.

d _____ es posible en este mundo.

e Temo que quieras a _____.

f _____ puede quererte como yo te quiero.

algunas	todo	cada
cualquier	otro	ninguno

13 **Corrige los ocho errores.**

Queremos que conozáis a Satcha Pretto, presentador de *Despierta América*.

Inició su carrera como presentadora de televisión en Texas y también era el voz

de *Primero Impacto* que se transmitaba los sábados y domingos. Ha ganada

premios importante incluyendo un Emmy.

14 **Lee este párrafo e identifica un ejemplo de cada categoría gramatical.**

Los inmigrantes están empezando a volverse a España, pero los españoles
no han dejado de emigrar. La población está todavía descendiendo, pero no
al ritmo que llevaba hace un par de años. Esto sugiere que la economía está
mejorando. Esperamos que el número de españoles obligados a emigrar
empiece a bajar este año.

perfect tense _____

present tense radical changing verb _____

reflexive verb _____

present continuous _____

imperfect tense _____

past participle _____

subjunctive _____

15 **Completa con la forma correcta de la palabra entre paréntesis.**

a Las medidas no eran muy _____. (*eficaz*)

b El agua estaba muy _____. (*frío*)

c Necesitaban _____ más casas. (*construir*)

d Mi padre insiste en que _____ a la universidad. (*ir*)

e La semana que viene nosotros _____ que ir. (*tener*)

f _____ el dinero en el sobre, por favor. (*poner*)

g Comimos en el restaurante y nos _____ mucho. (*gustar*)

h Es imposible que mis primos _____ este año. (*venir*)

i El presidente _____ anteayer que iban a buscar una solución. (*decir*)

j Es el _____ presidente elegido democráticamente. (*primero*)

k Oye, Juana. No _____ más, ya lo encontré. (*buscar*)

l Usted _____ la culpable de todas mis angustias. (*ser*)

1 Lee las palabras y sus definiciones. Escribe una traducción de la palabra en negrita.

a **Capilla**. Es una iglesia pequeña o parte de una catedral dedicada a un santo. _____

b **Papa**. Es el cabeza de la Iglesia Católica. Reside en el Vaticano. _____

c **Cáliz**. Es un tipo de vaso que se utiliza para celebrar la Misa. _____

d **Pecado**. Acción reprehensible que prohíbe la moralidad de la Iglesia. _____

e **Discípulo**. Seguidor del Mesías. _____

f **Convento**. Residencia de monjas. _____

g **Monasterio**. Comunidad de monjes. _____

h **Peregrino**. Viajero que visita importantes sitios religiosos. _____

i **Milagro**. Acontecimiento imposible realizado por el poder de Dios. _____

2 Escoge la mejor traducción de las palabras subrayadas.

a Es un plato típico de Valencia. *plate / dish*

b Se cayó en el barro. *mud / earthenware*

c Desempeñó un papel importante. *paper / role*

d Se sirvió en una olla de barro. *mud / earthenware*

e Su único paradero era un cartón debajo de un puente. *cardboard / box / card*

f Era un títere hecho de papel. *paper / role*

g Le entregaron su cartón para jugar al loto. *cardboard / box / card*

3 Traduce al inglés.

a España se compone de diecisiete comunidades autónomas.

_____

b Puebla es el nombre de una ciudad y también de un estado mexicano.

_____

c Los países de Inglaterra, Escocia, Irlanda del Norte y Gales se conocen como el Reino Unido.

_____

_____

d El rey unió la nación frente a la crisis.

_____

e Los guerreros cristianos reconquistaron la península ibérica.

_____

f Bajo los Reyes Católicos, Fernando e Isabel, los principales reinos de España se unificaron.

_____

_____

> ✅ **Consejo**
>
> Many of the concepts on this page will appear in the translations on pages 50 and 52.

4 Traduce al inglés.

Con la Navidad llega la tradición de romper las piñatas. La piñata es una olla de barro o de cartón que se cubre de papeles de colores. Contiene dulces, juguetes y fruta. <u>La piñata se cuelga para luego pegarla por turnos con un palo</u>. Las hay de varios diseños, desde burros a tortugas ninja. Pero la piñata navideña tiene siete picos para representar los siete pecados capitales.

_____

_____

_____

_____

_____

_____

_____

_____

> ✅ **Consejo**
>
> The underlined sentence will not translate word for word into English. Make sure you understand exactly what it says about what you do with a *piñata*. To explain it in good English you may need to change the sentence around. Be careful not to miss out anything or to add too much.

5 Traduce al inglés.

La gastronomía del estado de Puebla es reconocida no solo a nivel nacional, sino internacional, por la variedad de sus platos. Son recetas llenas de sabores, olores y colores. Con su origen en las cocinas de los conventos o de los hogares particulares, han llegado a difundirse por todo el país. El mejor ejemplo es el *mole poblano* con más de veinte ingredientes. Es uno de los orgullos culinarios de Puebla.

_____

_____

_____

_____

_____

_____

_____

> ✅ **Consejo**
>
> You won't be able to translate the word *orgullos* literally.

6 Traduce al inglés.

El Santo Grial se encuentra en una capilla de la Catedral de Valencia. Es un cáliz de piedra que data del siglo primero. La leyenda cuenta que después de la muerte de Cristo, sus pocas pertenencias personales se repartieron entre sus discípulos. Según la historia, San Pedro, el primer Papa, llevó el cáliz a Roma. En la Edad Media un Papa español lo llevó a Huesca, Aragón. A su vez, un rey de Aragón lo entregó a la Catedral. Es un testimonio importante de la continuidad del cristianismo en la península, vinculando el desarrollo de distintos reinos cristianos con el poder de la Iglesia, y su papel en la creación de una nación unida, compuesta de distintas comunidades autónomas.

_____

_____

_____

_____

_____

_____

> ✅ **Consejo**
>
> If you need help with the word *entregar*, have a look at activity 1 on page 51.

1 Escoge el verbo que reemplace al verbo *dar* en cada ejemplo. Escribe la forma correcta del verbo.

a   *I handed in my homework to my teacher.*

Di mis deberes a mi profesor. _____

b   *I gave him some socks as a present on his birthday.*

Le di unos calcetines en su cumpleaños. _____

c   *They are going to give him the title of best player.*

Le van a dar el título de mejor jugador. _____

d   *He gave them a million pesos for the project.*

Les dio un millón de pesos para el proyecto. _____

regalar	donar	entregar	conferir

> ☑ **Consejo**
>
> *Dar* is used in many idiomatic expressions, but in its literal meaning of 'give' you can often find a more precise word to use.

2 Escoge la palabra adecuada para hacer una traducción correcta.

a   She lived there until 1973.

Vivió allí **hasta / hasta que** 1973.

b   He lived there until he got married.

Vivió allí **hasta / hasta que** se casó.

c   They moved to Spain after the war.

Se mudaron a España **después de que / después de** la guerra.

d   They moved because of the war.

Se mudaron **porque / a causa de** la guerra.

e   He lived there after he got married.

Vivió allí **después de que / después de** se casara.

> ☑ **Consejo**
>
> Consider what comes next. Is it a noun or a clause with *que* and a verb?

3 Utiliza *dejar* o *quedarse* para traducir.

a   He left his country. _____

b   She stopped smoking. _____

c   He was left with all the money. _____

d   They didn't let him go. _____

4 Lee las definiciones y elige la traducción correcta de estas palabras.

Un caldo es un líquido claro que se puede utilizar para hacer sopa. Un guiso es cuando la carne se cocina en su propio líquido. Fideos son un tipo de pasta muy fina. El azafrán es una especia que viene de una flor y da un color amarillo. Las habichuelas o las alubias son las semillas blancas y grandes de las judías verdes.

a   stew _____

b   saffron _____

c   beans _____

d   noodles _____

e   stock _____

5 Traduce al español.

An 'aguinaldo' is a small bag of fruit or sweets which is given as a present at Christmas in Mexico. They are given to each guest on the occasion of 'posadas' when friends and family act out the arrival of the Holy Family looking for somewhere to stay. They sing songs and call at different houses looking for a room. In the last house they come to, the lights are turned on and everyone celebrates.

_____

_____

_____

_____

_____

_____

_____

✅ Consejo

The activities and texts on pages 49 and 50 will give you some support with these translations.

✅ Consejo

Take great care with 'the last house they come to'.

✅ Consejo

You can decide whether to use the passive voice or replace it with *se*.

6 Traduce al español.

Rice dishes are of great importance in Spanish national and regional identity. There are three basic types. 'Arroz caldoso' is served like a soup. 'Arroz meloso' has less liquid, but the rice is cooked until it is soft and smooth. 'Paella' is cooked until the rice is 'dry' and there is no stock left at all. In Cataluña the dish 'fideuá' is similar, but made with noodles instead of rice.

_____

_____

_____

_____

_____

_____

_____

✅ Consejo

Hasta que takes the subjunctive when it refers to something that hasn't happened yet.

7 Traduce al español.

The monastery of San Juan de la Peña is one of the most important monuments in Spain from the Middle Ages. It is associated with the legend of the birth of the Christian kingdom of Aragón and the start of the Reconquest of Spain. The warriors met here to choose their leader before the battle where a burning cross miraculously appeared in the sky. Many of the Kings of Aragón are buried in a chapel here. It is situated in a spectacular position under an enormous rock and extends into a cave. For many years the Holy Grail was kept here to attract pilgrims.

✅ Consejo

Decide if 'are buried' is a description of their current state (*estar*), or a statement of what happens to them (passive voice with *ser*). You can look at the text on page 32 to check.

_____

_____

_____

_____

_____

_____

_____

1 Completa estas frases con la forma correcta del verbo en el presente.

a Las tapas _____ típicas de España. (*ser*)

b En el norte _____ de bar en bar. (*ir*) (*tú*)

c En el sur _____ más común quedarse en un bar. (*ser*)

d _____ comido pinchos en San Sebastián. (*haber*) (*nosotros*)

e Los bares y restaurantes _____ en el casco histórico. (*estar*)

f El año que viene, _____ a Granada. (*ir*) (*nosotros*)

g Granada _____ en Andalucía. (*estar*)

2 Traduce al español.

a We go to Spain every year.

_____

b We have bought a house in Santander.

_____

c It is near the sea.

_____

d It is quite small.

_____

e My parents go there in the winter.

_____

f They are there now.

_____

Gramática

There are only four verbs that are completely irregular in the present tense, but they are very high frequency verbs:

ser:

soy	eres	es
somos	sois	son

estar:

estoy	estás	está
estamos	estáis	están

ir:

voy	vas	va
vamos	vais	van

haber:

he	has	ha
hemos	habéis	han

These verbs have an irregular form in the 1st person of the present tense:

ver – veo	*caber – quepo*
dar – doy	*caer – caigo*
saber – sé	*traer – traigo*

See page 9 for regular verbs in the present tense and verbs with *g* or *zc* in the 1st person form.

See page 15 for radical changing verbs in the present tense.

See page 23 for the perfect tense using *haber*.

3 Corrige los ocho errores de este texto.

La gastronomía se a convertido en uno de los atractivos principales del norte de España. San Sebastián se la ciudad que más estrellas Michelin a recibido por número de habitantes. Habemos visitado varios bares y puedo decir que los pinchos ser deliciosos. Si ir al barrio histórico estas rodeado de diferentes bares y la variedad y la calidad ser fantásticas.

4 Traduce al español.

Tapas are typical of Spanish cuisine. If you go to a bar you can order a 'ración' or a 'tapa'. If you are all going to share, it is best to order a 'ración'. So, if you are in Spain and you have never tried tapas, it is an experience that I recommend.

_____

_____

_____

_____

_____

1 Subraya los verbos en el pretérito. Pon un círculo alrededor de los verbos en el imperfecto.

a Trabajaba demasiado y le dio un ataque de estrés y depresión.

b Comía mucha comida rápida pero de repente decidió mejorar su dieta.

c Empezó a cuidarse porque su salud corría peligro.

d Fue mi cumpleaños y estaba enferma.

e Comía demasiado pero dejó de beber alcohol.

f Pasó un día entero en la cama pero no dormía bien.

g Veía la televisión y jugaba con la tableta.

h Sus padres no ayudaron y hacían comentarios de mal gusto.

2 Lee el texto. Pon una (P) sobre los verbos que requieren el pretérito y pon una (I) sobre los que requieren el imperfecto en una traducción al español.

The Spanish used to eat a diet of national food but all that changed. In the past they used to eat healthily but in more recent times they started to eat processed foods. Many Spanish people used to eat out a lot so when the diet changed they found themselves eating too much.

3 Ahora completa la traducción del texto de la actividad 2.

Los españoles (*comer*) ᵃ _____ una dieta de comida

autóctona, pero todo eso (*cambiar*) ᵇ _____. En

el pasado (*comer*) ᶜ _____ comida sana, pero en

tiempos más recientes, cuando (*ponerse*) ᵈ _____ de

moda los restaurantes de comida rápida (*empezar*) ᵉ _____

a comer comida procesada. Muchos españoles (*comer*) ᶠ _____

en la calle así que cuando (*cambiar*) ᵍ _____ su dieta,

(*encontrarse*) ʰ _____ comiendo demasiado.

4 Completa la traducción, poniendo el tiempo verbal adecuado de las palabras subrayadas.

My grandparents live in Barcelona but when they were young they lived in the countryside. Their life was very different. Every day they went to the little primary school in the morning and in the afternoons they helped their parents in the house or in the fields. On Sundays they went to church.

Mis abuelos viven en Barcelona pero cuando (*ser*) ᵃ _____ jóvenes

(*vivir*) ᵇ _____ en el campo. Su vida era muy diferente. Cada día (*ir*)

ᶜ _____ a la pequeña escuela por la mañana y por la tarde (*ayudar*)

ᵈ _____ a sus padres en la casa o en el campo. El domingo (*ir*)

ᵉ _____ a misa.

⚑ Gramática

Look at the explanation of when to use the preterite and imperfect tenses on pages 10 and 11.

⚑ Gramática

Sometimes you cannot rely on the English form to tell you which tense to use. You may need to use the imperfect in Spanish even when in English we don't say 'used to' or 'was -ing'.

When I was young I played a lot of tennis. *Cuando era joven jugaba mucho al tenis.*

I couldn't get out of bed because I had a headache. *No podía levantarme porque tenía dolor de cabeza.*

When I was small, I would go down to the river and catch fish. *Cuando era joven iba al río y pescaba.*

1 ¿Cuál es el infinitivo de estos verbos?

a murió _____

b confirieron _____

c riñeron _____

d sintió _____

e pidieron _____

f durmieron _____

g sonrió _____

Gramática

All radical changing -ir verbs in the present tense also change their stem in the 3rd person singular and plural in the preterite tense.

preferir:
*preferí   preferiste   prefirió
preferimos   preferisteis   prefirieron*

See page 10 for regular verbs in the preterite tense.

See page 15 for radical changing verbs.

2 Escribe el verbo completo en el pretérito.

dormir

	dormimos
dormiste	

3 Traduce al español.

a It frightened me. _____

b We hurried. _____

c They didn't give me time. _____

d We went home. _____

e It was a disaster. _____

4 Escribe en español.

a We asked for the bill. _____

b She asked for help. _____

c We realised. _____

d It was my brother. _____

e They slept. _____

f I slept. _____

g I didn't realise. _____

Consejo

Remember that the verb *dar* is used in expressions such as:

me da miedo – it frightens me

me da frío – it makes me feel cold

5 Completa estas frases con la forma correcta del verbo en el pretérito.

a Mi hermano _____ en la calle y le _____ frío. (*dormir, dar*)

b Los malos de la película _____ pero nadie _____. (*reñir, morir*)

c El soldado _____ que era muy tarde para estar en la calle. (*sentir*)

d El policía nos dijo adónde _____ los prisioneros. (*ir*)

e Mi hermana _____ a Estados Unidos porque _____ con mi padre. (*ir, reñir*)

f Nosotros _____ mucho. (*reírse*)

Gramática

There are only three completely irregular verbs in the preterite tense. They have an irregular stem and irregular endings.

dar:
*di   diste   dio
dimos   disteis   dieron*

ir:
*fui   fuiste   fue
fuimos   fuisteis fueron*

ser:
*fui   fuiste   fue
fuimos   fuisteis fueron*

Notice *ir* and *ser* share the same preterite form.

See page 19 for the group of verbs known as the strong preterite.

1 Completa la traducción.

a He ido a ver un tablao flamenco.

_____ _to see a flamenco performance._

b Están tocando la guitarra y cantando.

_____ _the guitar and singing._

c Han bailado un fandango.

_____ _a fandango._

d Me estoy divirtiendo.

_____ _myself._

e He aprendido mucho.

_____ _a lot._

Gramática

Tenses made up of more than one part, an auxiliary verb and a participle, are compound tenses.

See page 18 for continuous tenses using _estar_ plus present participle.

See page 23 for the perfect tense using _haber_ plus past participle.

2 Completa con la forma correcta del verbo.

a Han _____ al barrio de Sacromonte de Granada. (_subir_)

b Están _____ las famosas cuevas. (_buscar_)

c Ellos _____ oído hablar de un cantaor famoso.

d Él _____ cantando esta noche en un tablao.

e _____ vuelto a su ciudad natal.

Gramática

Some linguists consider that the perfect and continuous forms are not strictly speaking tenses, since they are built out of the simple tenses of _estar_ and _haber_. This is because they can be re-combined in flexible ways and it becomes artificial to label each one as a new tense.

He estado pensando. (I have been thinking.)

Habría estado comiendo. (I would have been eating.)

Después de haber estado trabajando (After having been working)

3 Lee y traduce los verbos subrayados al inglés.

Si tienes la suerte de conocer la peña Cardamomo, <u>habrás estado visitando</u> uno de los mejores lugares para disfrutar de una noche mágica de música y baile. <u>Habíamos estado pasando</u> unos momentos inolvidables cuando de repente, uno de los hombres que <u>había estado escuchando</u> al lado de nosotros entre el público, se levantó y se puso a bailar. <u>Habíamos estado compartiendo</u> una mesa con Antonio Gades, uno de los mejores bailaores del mundo. <u>Después de haber estado disfrutando</u> toda la noche, fuimos a desayunar una tortilla antes de acostarnos.

_____

_____

_____

_____

_____

_____

_____

4 Traduce al español.

a I have been playing the guitar. _____

b He will have been singing. _____

c We would have been listening. _____

d They had been dancing. _____

1 Identifica el pronombre directo (D) y el indirecto (I).

a El profesor estaba explicando el subjuntivo. Nos lo explicaba en español.

b Fui a ver una obra de arte. El artista me la enseñó.

c El músico tocaba una canción. Me la cantó en inglés.

d El escritor puede expresártelo mejor que yo.

2 Completa la traducción.

a *I went to the shop to buy some paint brushes. They sold them to me.*

Fui a la tienda para comprar unos pinceles. _____

b *My boyfriend was reading a poem. He dedicated it to me.*

Mi novio leía un poema. (*dedicar*) _____

c *Listen to the teacher. He will explain it to you.*

Escucha al profesor. _____

> ### 🔧 Gramática
>
> Where two pronouns together would produce the combinations
> *le lo, le la, le las, le los*, the *le* changes to *se*.
> *Se lo dije.* (I told him it.)
> *Dáselo.* (Give him it.)

3 Completa con los pronombres correctos.

a Su guitarra estaba desafinada. El profesor _____ afinó.

b Ana no conocía los pasos del baile. El maestro _____ mostró.

c Mi hermano quería un DVD. _____ compré.

d Querían tres entradas. _____ vendieron.

se	se	lo	los
se	se	la	las

4 Traduce al español.

a She has some great songs. She sang them to me.

_____

b I like his poems. He read them to us.

_____

c I had a question. So I asked her it.

_____

d I needed a photo. He took it for me.

_____

e You like the DVD. I will buy it for you.

_____

f I like the DVD. Buy it for me.

_____

> ### 🔧 Gramática
>
> See page 35 for direct object pronouns.
> See page 36 for indirect object pronouns.
> When a verb takes an indirect and a direct object pronoun, the indirect object pronoun **always** goes first.
> *Me lo dijo.* (He told it to me.)
> *Voy a decírselo.* (I am going to tell him it.)
> When the pronouns go on the end of an infinitive, imperative or present participle, an accent is needed to keep the stress in the correct place.
> *Dámelo.* (Give it to me.)
> *Voy a dártelo.* (I'm going to give it to you.)
> *Estoy enseñándotelo.* (I am showing it to you.)
> In this example with the present continuous, it is easier to put the pronouns in front of the conjugated verb *estar*.
> *Te lo estoy enseñando.*

> ### 🔧 Gramática
>
> The personal *a* is used when the direct object of a verb is a person.
> *Laura vio **a** mi tío en la calle.*
> The *a* does not mean the object becomes an indirect object.
> *Laura vio a mi tío en la calle.* Ë *Laura **lo** vio en la calle.*

1 Convierte estos adjetivos en adverbios.

Ejemplo: completo → _completa_ → _completamente_

a cuidadoso _____ _____

b peligroso _____ _____

c especial _____ _____

d natural _____ _____

e simpático _____ _____

f afortunado _____ _____

g desalentador _____ _____

2 Lee e identifica los adverbios. ¿Cómo podrías modificar el texto para evitar tanta repetición de -*mente*?

Es un lugar de gran encanto natural donde las especies amenazadas viven tranquilamente y sin peligro de caer en manos de los cazadores que paulatinamente acaban con la fauna de otros lugares. Claramente debemos actuar consistentemente para proteger ese enclave.

_____

_____

_____

_____

_____

3 Subraya los cinco adjetivos. Pon un círculo alrededor de los tres adverbios.

La reserva natural de Doñana está en gran peligro de secarse rápidamente.

Las autoridades deben actuar inmediatamente para evitar que la extracción

de demasiada agua subterránea haga daños irreparables, antes de que sea

demasiado tarde.

4 Traduce al español.

The effect of constant extraction of water is badly interpreted, but inevitably dries up the nature reserve.

_____

_____

_____

_____

⚡ Gramática

Adverbs are formed by taking the feminine form of an adjective and adding -*mente*.

If an adjective has an accent, it is still needed in the adverb.

Some adjectives do not have a feminine form so -*mente* is added to the masculine form.

rápido → _rápidamente_

normal → _normalmente_

Where a clause has two or more adverbs, Spanish puts -*mente* on the final adverb but drops it on the others:

Comía ruidos**a**, rápid**a** y groser**amente**.

Sometimes an adverb feels clumsy, so it is better to use an adverbial phrase:

injustamente – de forma injusta

inequitativamente – de manera inequitativa

⚡ Gramática

As well as modifying a verb, an adverb can be used to modify an adjective.

Es completamente imposible.

This includes adverbs like _demasiado_, _bien_ or _mal_ which don't end in -*mente*.

☑ Consejo

When words like _demasiado_ are adjectives they have to agree for gender and number.

Adjective agreeing with the noun it is describing:

Hay demasiados turistas.

When they are adverbs, they do not agree with the noun.

Adverb modifying the adjective:

Los turistas son demasiado groseros.

1 Haz una lista de estas palabras y di cuál es su significado más común en inglés. Hay dos significados de *a, en* y *de*.

a	a	**f**	hacia	**k**	encima de
b	en	**g**	desde	**l**	sobre
c	de	**h**	hasta	**m**	entre
d	con	**i**	debajo de	**n**	al lado de
e	sin	**j**	dentro de	**o**	después de

> ### Gramática
> Prepositions may or may not translate literally from English to Spanish.
>
> English often uses a two-word verb plus preposition construction, where Spanish uses a single verb.
>
> *entrar* (to go in)
>
> *salir* (to go out)
>
> See page 14 for Spanish verbs which take a preposition plus the infinitive.

2 Traduce estas frases al inglés.

a Fui a pie. _____

b Estaba de pie. _____

c Lo hice a mano. _____

d Lo hizo a su manera. _____

e Estaba pensando en ti. _____

f Soñé con mi abuela anoche. _____

3 Empareja las frases en inglés (a–f) con las frases en español (i–vi) .

a	to look for	**i**	separar
b	to wait for	**ii**	esperar
c	to fall out	**iii**	pelearse
d	to wake up	**iv**	buscar
e	to think up	**v**	despertarse
f	to break up	**vi**	imaginar

4 Traduce al inglés.

a Iba a comprar un regalo para mi sobrina.

_____

b Cuando viajaba por la carretera, el coche que iba delante se averió.

_____

c Por mala suerte chocamos.

_____

d Por lo visto, fue un simple accidente.

_____

e Por lo menos nadie se hizo daño.

_____

f No pude ir a comprar el regalo, así que mi tío compró uno por mí.

_____

> ### Gramática
> The words *por* and *para* can both be translated as 'for'.
>
> 'For' usually means 'in order to', 'destined for', 'intended for'. Spanish uses *para* for all these most common uses.
>
> *Fui a España para aprender. El avión para Madrid. Lo compré para ti.*
>
> Most of the time *por* isn't translated as 'for'. It can mean 'by' or 'through' or appear in a range of fixed expressions.
>
> *un libro escrito por García Márquez*
>
> *envía la carta por correo*
>
> *por accidente*
>
> *por el parque*
>
> *por cierto*
>
> *por completo*
>
> *por desgracia*
>
> *por favor*
>
> *por fin*
>
> When *por* can be translated as 'for' it means 'in exchange for', 'on behalf of' or 'caused by'.
>
> *Lo cambié por otro. Lo hice por el bien de la humanidad. Murió por falta de agua.*

1 **Completa la traducción.**

a *I did it for him.* Lo hice para _____.

b *He took a photo of me.* Me sacó una foto a _____.

c *They went with us.* Fueron _____.

d *To him, it seemed fine.* _____ le pareció bien.

e *He sat down next to her.* Se sentó al lado de _____.

f *She said it to you.* Te lo dijo a _____.

> **Gramática**
>
> In Spain (but not in all Spanish-speaking countries) a preposition is not followed directly by the word 'which'. The correct form of the word 'the' comes between the preposition and *que* or *cual*.
> *El coche en el cual llegué.*
> *Los amigos con los cuales estaba hablando.*
> *La situación en la que me encuentro.*
> With *quien / quienes* you must not do this.
> *La persona con quien vivo.*
> *Los amigos a quienes he escrito.*

> **Gramática**
>
> Disjunctive pronouns follow a preposition:
> *para mí, a mí, en mí, de mí*
> The pronouns are:
> *mí, ti, él/ella/ello, nosotros/nosotras, vosotros/vosotras, ellos/ellas*
> The preposition *con* has an irregular composite form:
> *conmigo* (with me) *contigo* (with you)
> The other persons are normal:
> *con él, con nosotros, con vosotros, con ellos*
> There is a reflexive 3rd person form:
> *lo llevó consigo* (he took it with him(self))
> The disjunctive pronoun *él* does not shorten to *al* after the preposition *a*.
> *No le llamaron a él.*

2 **Escribe la palabra *el/la/los/las* en el lugar adecuado.**

a Es importante tener una novia en cual tener confianza.

b Ellos son los amigos para cuales hice tantos esfuerzos.

c Es la casa en que nací.

d Eres la persona con que escojo pasar mi vida.

e Vimos al hombre a que habíamos dado el dinero.

f Ayudamos a una niña a que habían operado.

3 **Traduce al español.**

a It is less important to ask what they can do for us…

_____

b than to ask what we can do for them.

_____

c There are agencies in whom they can trust.

_____

d For me it is the most difficult thing.

_____

e There are situations it is easy to get into…

_____

f but from which it is difficult to get out.

_____

> **Consejo**
>
> In some Spanish-speaking countries *de mí* sounds wrong. You will see alternative ways of avoiding it, even though it is perfectly correct.
> *Una foto de mí. Una foto mía.*
> *Al lado de mí. A mi lado.*

1 Traduce al español.

a **i** They gave him a bag of fruit as a present. _____

ii They gave it as a present. _____

iii They gave it to him. _____

b **i** They told the story to us. _____

ii They told us it. _____

c **i** He made a paella for me. _____

ii He made it. _____

iii He made it for me. _____

2 Completa estas frases con la forma correcta del verbo en el presente: *ir*, *ser*, *estar* o *haber*.

a La siesta _____ un estereotipo de España. (*ser*)

b Los españoles _____ a casa a mediodía. (*ir*)

c _____ allí con tu familia un par de horas. (*estar, tú*)

d Si _____ dormido a mediodía, puedo trabajar hasta las nueve de la noche. (*haber, yo*)

e No _____ perezosos. Trabajamos también por la tarde. (*ser, nosotros*)

3 Subraya los verbos en el pretérito. Pon un círculo alrededor de los verbos en el imperfecto.

a Participaba a una manifestación y la policía la detuvo.

b La policía obligó a los estudiantes a volver a la plaza donde se reunían.

c Los estudiantes quisieron dispersarse, pero los mantenían allí los coches patrulla.

d La prensa informó que la policía maltrataba a algunos de los manifestantes.

e Una señora mayor pasaba por la plaza y fue herida por una botella.

4 Traduce los verbos que has identificado en la actividad 3. Debes tener en cuenta la persona y el tiempo.

_____

_____

_____

_____

_____

_____

_____

_____

_____

_____

5 Completa estas frases con la forma correcta del verbo en el pretérito.

a Los obreros en huelga _____ la plaza. (*ocupar*)

b Unos policías armados _____ a negociar. (*ir*)

c Los líderes de los sindicatos _____ no hablar con ellos. (*preferir*)

d El alcalde _____ en la televisión. (*salir*)

e _____ y _____ que todo sería resuelto. (*sonreír*) (*decir*)

f Hubo algunas peleas, pero nadie _____. (*morir*)

g La policía _____ a varios. (*detener*)

6 Traduce al inglés.

a Quería salir con mi esposa para ir de tapas.

b Caminábamos por la calle buscando un bar de tapas.

c Había por lo menos cincuenta personas en cada bar.

d Por lo visto, es un barrio muy popular.

e Quería llamar a un restaurante para hacer una reserva.

f Por desgracia mi teléfono no funcionaba.

g Así que mi esposa hizo la llamada por mí.

_____

_____

_____

_____

_____

_____

_____

7 Ahora tapa a–g de la actividad 6. Vuelve a traducir tus frases al español poniendo atención en *por* y *para*.

a _____

b _____

c _____

d _____

e _____

f _____

g _____

8 Traduce estas frases al español en una hoja de papel aparte.

a It is very important to know that the regions of Spain have their own identity.

b Sometimes local identity is stronger than national identity.

c The most indispensable thing is to have institutions in which you can trust.

d It is less easy to trust an institution in Madrid.

e It is good to have someone to blame.

9 Completa la traducción con el pronombre correcto.

a *He stood in front of me.*

Se puso de pie delante de _____.

b *He sat next to us.*

Se sentó al lado de _____.

c *He went with me.*

Fue _____.

d *She went instead of us.*

Fue en vez de _____.

e *That house is ours.*

Esa casa es _____.

f *I saw him.*

_____ vi.

g *I told him.*

_____ dije.

h *I was thinking of you.*

Pensaba en _____.

10 Completa estas frases con los adverbios indicados.

a _____ me acuesto temprano.
(*normally*)

b Baila _____ y _____

_____. (*slowly, elegantly*)

c Escribes muy _____. (*well*)

d Ella es _____ trabajadora. (*too*)

e Conduce _____ que tú. (*better*)

f Habló con ellos _____. (*individually*)

11 Traduce al español.

a My mother wants you to come to dinner.

_____

b I don't care if you come or not.

_____

c I would prefer to go out.

_____

d You can decide what to tell her.

_____

e Don't tell her it is my idea.

_____

f I haven't told her anything.

_____

g I don't believe she knows.

_____

✅ **Consejo**

This activity is testing if you are still on top of a mixture of things from the book so far. Try to spot what each one is testing before you answer.

12 Completa la tabla con la forma correcta de los verbos.

	presente – yo	pretérito – yo	pretérito – él	imperfecto – yo	participio pasado	futuro – él
ser						
hacer						
volver						
morir						
ir						
conocer						
estar						
decir						
hablar						
comer						

13 Indica cuáles son las formas irregulares.

14 Traduce al español, escribiendo la forma correcta del verbo.

a   He introduced _____ (*introducir*)

b   They said _____ (*decir*)

c   I maintain _____ (*mantener*)

d   They have discovered _____ (*descubrir*)

e   They imposed _____ (*imponer*)

f   He would prefer _____ (*preferir*)

g   I saw _____ (*ver*)

h   He was walking _____ (*pasear*)

i   I played _____ (*jugar*)

✅ **Consejo**

In activity 14, make sure you identify what might catch you out about each verb.

1 Lee la frase y traduce mejor la palabra subrayada.

a Rompió un número importante de ventanas.

He broke an important number of windows. _____

b Voy a seguir viviendo en España.

I am going to follow living in Spain. _____

c Yo sí practico la siesta.

I do practise the siesta. _____

d Vi al policía en la calle.

I saw the police in the street. _____

e La paella es un tópico de la comida española.

Paella is a topic of Spanish food. _____

f Claro, es una buena idea.

Clear, it's a good idea. _____

g Provocó muchos destrozos.

It provoked a lot of destructions. _____

_____

> **✓ Consejo**
>
> Don't go for a literal translation if it doesn't make sense in English.

2 Traduce estas frases al inglés poniendo atención en el orden de las palabras.

a ¿Sabes de dónde son?

_____

b Tengo unos amigos con los cuales puedo reunirme.

_____

c La mayoría de los españoles suelen acostarse muy tarde.

_____

d Según dice mi mamá, no duermo lo suficiente.

_____

e Participaron treinta jóvenes en la protesta.

_____

3 Escribe una mejor traducción para estas frases.

a En vez de acostarme fui de fiesta.

Instead of to go to bed, I went to party. _____

b A la niña le causó mucha tristeza.

To the girl it caused her a lot of sadness. _____

c Antes de llegar comimos algo.

Before to arrive we ate something. _____

d A mí me aburre eso.

To me that bores me. _____

e Mi profesor es muy bueno corriendo.

My teacher is very good running. _____

f Me interesa estudiar.

I am interested in to study. _____

4 Traduce al inglés.

La región de La Mancha se conoce por tres cosas: el ingenioso hidalgo Don Quijote, el queso manchego y el director de cine Pedro Almodóvar. Por supuesto, hay que conocer más que estos tres tópicos populares, pero si uno solo conoce estos, entonces ya sabe algo de La Mancha. Conoce sus pueblos aislados, su paisaje, sus molinos, es consciente de sus tradiciones y creencias, adivina la vida del pastor y los rigores de la trashumancia de las ovejas y respeta el ingenio (y el genio) de sus habitantes.

✓ **Consejo**

Decide how you are going to translate *uno* and then stick to your decision.

_____

_____

_____

_____

_____

_____

_____

_____

_____

5 Traduce al inglés.

Los españoles están considerando abolir la siesta. Descansar por la tarde representa horas perdidas que luego los obliga a seguir en el trabajo hasta las nueve de la noche. La mayoría de los trabajadores ya no tienen la oportunidad de volver a casa para aprovechar sus dos horas libres a mediodía. Trabajar hasta las nueve implica cenar a las diez y ver la televisión hasta medianoche. El veinticinco por ciento de los españoles confiesa trasnochar rutinariamente.

✓ **Consejo**

English and Spanish have different ideas of 'afternoon', 'evening' and 'night'. Make sure your translation is in good English.

✓ **Consejo**

An infinitive can be translated as 'to do' something, but also as 'doing' something.

_____

_____

_____

_____

_____

_____

6 Traduce al inglés.

Treinta jóvenes que participaron en una protesta antifascista fueron detenidos por varios policías de la Policía Nacional. Los habían obligado a volver hacia la Plaza de España, lo que llevó al enfrentamiento. Se lanzaron botellas y piedras a los coches patrulla y se provocaron importantes destrozos en el mobiliario urbano como contenedores de basura quemados, papeleras arrancadas o marquesinas rotas. Según explicó un portavoz, la actuación de la policía obedeció en todo momento al intento de proteger la manifestación de la Falange en la que participaron unos trescientos jóvenes y la cual había sido autorizada.

✓ **Consejo**

If you are unsure of how to translate names of places or cultural bodies, you can use the Spanish term and then give a translation or brief definition.

_____

_____

_____

_____

_____

_____

_____

_____

1 ¿Cómo se escribe en español?

a architecture _____

b archaeology _____

c technology _____

d immigration _____

e inhabitants _____

f to realise _____

g second _____

h unacceptable _____

i the mayor _____

j responsible _____

k appearance _____

l population _____

2 Escoge entre las dos palabras de cada frase.

a *The teacher gave a demonstration of the process.*

El profesor hizo **una demostración** / **una manifestación** del proceso.

b *The students took part in a political demonstration.*

Los estudiantes participaron en una **demostración** / **una manifestación** política.

c *The police said it was a peaceful protest.*

La policía dijo que fue una protesta **tranquila** / **pacífica**.

d *I spent a peaceful afternoon by the river.*

Pasé una tarde muy **tranquila** / **pacífica** al lado del río.

e *The policeman arrested him.*

El policía / **La policía** lo detuvo.

f *The police arrested him.*

El policía / **La policía** lo detuvo.

3 Escoge el verbo adecuado para completar la traducción.

a *Nobody knows what is happening.*

Nadie _____ qué está pasando.

b *Everyone knows him.*

Todos lo _____.

c *In the square I can meet up with my friends.*

En la plaza puedo _____ con mis amigas.

d *My grandparents met in Barcelona.*

Mis abuelos se _____ en Barcelona.

e *You need to find a good lawyer.*

Necesitas _____ un buen abogado.

f *He recognised me immediately.*

Me _____ de inmediato.

g *He arrives without you realising.*

Llega sin que _____.

h *We are aware of the dangers.*

_____ de los peligros.

conocen	reconoció	somos conscientes	sabe
conocieron	encontrar	te des cuenta	encontrarme

> ✅ **Consejo**
>
> Some of the activities and texts on pages 65 and 66 will help you with these translations.

4 Traduce al español.

Everyone knows what the clichés of Andalusian culture are. But of course we all realise that there is more to get to know. It is ridiculous for you to think that all the inhabitants spend their time playing the guitar or listening to Paco Peña. It is not a region which lives in the past. In fact the oldest archaeological site in Spain, Marroquíes Bajos in Jaén, has been turned into a housing estate.

_____

_____

_____

_____

_____

> ✅ **Consejo**
>
> Watch out for subjunctives:
>
> following a value judgement (it is … that …)
>
> implying that what someone thinks is wrong (you can't think that …)
>
> following a negative antecedent (not … which …)

5 Traduce al español.

The siesta is a cliché of the life of Spanish people. Traditionally the day has been divided in two, with five hours' work in the morning, then, after lunch and a siesta, a return to work, often until eight or nine at night. It means that when most workers in other countries are coming out of work at around five in the afternoon, the Spanish are only just starting the second part of the day.

_____

_____

_____

_____

_____

6 Traduce al español.

A protest of young people demonstrating against immigration has been broken up by the National Police. The demonstration was not violent, but it did not have official authorisation. A spokesperson said that the police do not take into account the opinions being expressed, as long as they are within the law. In this case no arrests were made as the protesters negotiated with the police and dispersed willingly. The mayor has said that it is unacceptable that such protests should be allowed, but the police say that if permission is granted, a peaceful protest could take place.

_____

_____

_____

_____

_____

_____

_____

1 Una frase tiene un verbo en el subjuntivo. Subraya ese verbo. Explica la diferencia entre las dos frases.

   i   Cuando voy a España me quedo en la casa de mis tíos.

   ii Cuando vaya a España iré a Madrid.

2 Completa la traducción al inglés.

   a Cuando hayan terminado la restauración, será una obra de arte de las más importantes.

      When _____

   b En cuanto llegue, dile que me llame.

      As soon as _____

   c Cuando vayas a Granada, tendrás que visitar la Alhambra.

      When _____

   d El día que te cases, yo me comprometo a estar allí.

      The day _____

   e Hasta que pague, no podrá entrar.

      Until _____

   f Después de que se vayan, limpiaremos la casa.

      After _____

⭐ 3 Decide si se puede usar el subjuntivo o no.

   a Cuando **vamos** / **vayamos** a la playa vamos a Cala del Pi.

   b Cuando **voy** / **vaya** a España me alojaré en un hotel de lujo.

   c Cuando **entra** / **entre** el director, nos ponemos a trabajar inmediatamente.

   d Cuando **viene** / **venga** tu mamá le preguntaremos.

   e Cuando **nieve** / **nieva**, volved a la casa.

⭐ 4 Traduce al español utilizando el subjuntivo. Luego completa la frase con tus propias ideas.

   Ejemplo: Cuando vaya a España, *iré a Madrid*.

   a When I am thirty _____

      _____

   b When I go to Argentina _____

      _____

   c As soon as I have my own house _____

      _____

   d The day I finish school _____

      _____

   e As soon as you buy a new computer _____

      _____

   f When women have equal rights _____

      _____

🔂 Gramática

When referring to the future, a sentence may contain a clause which is not true (yet) and might not happen.

E.g. When **I am sixty**.

The words in capitals are hypothetical. This clause will therefore require the present subjunctive in Spanish.

cuando sea mayor (when I am older)

cuando mi hermano tenga ocho años (when my brother is eight)

✅ Consejo

Clauses introduced by *cuando* or *que* and referring to the future can take the subjunctive.

Sentences in the present tense with *si* do not.

Si voy a España, iré a Valencia.

---

1 Una de las frases tiene un verbo en el subjuntivo. Subraya este verbo. Explica la diferencia entre las dos frases.

a **i** Trabajo mucho para aprender a hablar español.

 ii El profesor trabaja mucho para que aprendamos español.

 _____

b **i** Entra sin que nadie te vea, si puedes.

 ii Entró sin hablar.

 _____

c **i** Antes de irse fue al baño.

 ii Antes de que te vayas, ve al baño.

 _____

d **i** Después de que se haya dormido, hablaremos de eso.

 ii Después de dormir, hablaremos de eso.

 _____

⭐ **2** Completa la traducción con la forma correcta del verbo en el subjuntivo.

Before Jaime goes, he has to help us in order for us all to do our homework. If we leave here without him explaining how to do it, it will be impossible. Unless he sends us an email.

Antes de que Jaime se (*ir*) ᵃ _____ , tiene que ayudarnos para que

todos (*hacer*) ᵇ _____ nuestros deberes. Si nos vamos de aquí sin que

nos (*explicar*) ᶜ _____ cómo hacerlo, será imposible. A menos que nos

(*enviar*) ᵈ _____ un correo electrónico.

3 Traduce al inglés.

a España será siempre una monarquía, a menos que ocurra algún escándalo.

 _____

b Hacemos sacrificios para que nuestros hijos tengan una vida mejor.

 _____

c Vamos a hacerlo, sin que nos digan cómo lo tenemos que hacer.

 _____

d Antes de que sea demasiado tarde, hay que actuar ahora.

 _____

⭐ **4** Traduce al español.

a So that the sick children can survive, we are asking for money.

 _____

b Before the programme ends, write down this number.

 _____

c Unless you have a better idea, we will not go.

 _____

d Provided that he helps us, everything will be fine.

 _____

e We can't do it without him supporting us.

 _____

🔲 Gramática

Some expressions are always followed by the subjunctive.

They can be similar to *quiero que* + subjunctive but do not contain a verb. (See page 38.)

Quiero que saques buenas notas. (I want you to get good grades.)

para que *saques buenas notas* (in order that you get good grades)

sin que *saques buenas notas* (without you getting good grades)

Some are similar to the subjunctive of futurity, referring to actions that may not happen. (See page 69.)

cuando *llegue* (when he arrives)

con tal de que *llegue* (provided he arrives)

a menos que *llegue* (unless he arrives)

antes de que *llegue* (before he arrives)

⬛ Gramática

To form the stem of the imperfect subjunctive, take the 3rd person plural of the preterite.

hablar – hablaron – hablara

comer – comieron – comiera

tener – tuvieron – tuviera

Use these endings for the imperfect subjunctive:

-*ar* verbs

habl**ara**	habl**aras**	habl**ara**
habl**áramos**	habl**arais**	habl**aran**

-*er*/-*ir* verbs

com**iera**	com**ieras**	com**iera**
com**iéramos**	com**ierais**	com**ieran**

You may see the alternative form for endings in the imperfect subjunctive:

hablase

comiese

✅ Consejo

The imperfect subjunctive is used in the same way as the present subjunctive (see page 38), but referring to the past.

1 Doubt/Improbability:

No sabía que tuviera dinero. (I didn't know that he had any money.)

Era poco probable que viniera. (It was unlikely that he would come.)

2 Value judgement/Emotion:

Era genial que ganáramos. (It was great that we won.)

Fue chocante que muriera. (It was shocking that he died.)

3 Wanting someone else to do something:

Mis padres querían que vinieras. (My parents wanted you to come.)

Los jóvenes insistieron en que les escucharan. (The young people insisted that they listen to them.)

---

1 Indica cuáles están en el subjuntivo (S) y cuáles en el indicativo (I).

a   Pensé que era muy divertido. __

b   Quería que le ayudara. __

c   No pensé que fuera útil. __

d   Quería ir al concierto. __

e   Fue importante que me ayudaras. __

f   Los jóvenes tenían muchas responsabilidades. __

g   No creía que tuviéramos muchos deberes. __

2 Completa estas frases con el verbo en el subjuntivo.

a   No quería que _____ tus deberes. (*olvidar*)

b   Era importante que todos vosotros _____ buenas notas. (*sacar*)

c   No creía que _____ difícil. (*ser*)

d   Necesitaba que tú me _____. (*apoyar*)

e   No les gustó que los adultos les _____ qué hacer. (*decir*)

✅ Consejo

Remember to work out if a verb is -*ar*, -*er* or -*ir* before putting it into the imperfect subjunctive.

3 Cambia estas frases al pasado.

a   Necesita que le ayuden.

  Necesitaba que le _____.

b   Insiste en que hagamos los deberes.

  Insistió en que _____.

c   No es verdad que sea imposible.

  No era verdad que _____.

d   No quiero que sufra.

  No quería que _____.

e   No permiten que les diga nada.

  No permitieron que les _____ nada.

1 Empareja las dos mitades de las frases.

a Si lloviera demasiado

b Si perdiera el partido

c Si hiciera todos los deberes

d Si cambiaran la música

e Si tuviéramos más dinero

i más gente bailaría.

ii tendría que ganar los dos siguientes.

iii la fiesta se pospondría al otro día.

iv tendría más éxito en sus exámenes.

v podríamos independizarnos de nuestros padres.

> **Gramática**
>
> You will often meet the imperfect subjunctive in hypothetical sentences with 'if'.
>
> *si tuviera la oportunidad* (if I were to have the opportunity / if I had the opportunity)
>
> *si pudiera* (if I could)
>
> *si fuera* (if I were)

> **Consejo**
>
> Check page 12 to remind yourself how to say what 'would happen', using the conditional.

2 Completa la traducción.

a *I think about what would happen if I were to be in that situation.*

Pienso en qué _____ si _____ en esa situación. (*pasar, estar*)

b *Imagine what would happen if the King were to commit a crime.*

Imagina qué _____ si el rey _____ un delito. (*ocurrir, cometer*)

c *If you saw a child who needed help, you would support them.*

Si _____ a un niño que necesitaba ayuda, lo _____. (*ver, apoyar*)

d *If I were to face that situation, I don't know what I would do.*

Si me _____ a esa situación, no sé qué _____. (*enfrentar, hacer*)

3 Traduce al inglés.

a Si tuviera el dinero, iría a España.

_____

b Si fuera a España me alojaría en un hotel de lujo.

_____

c Si me alojara en un hotel de lujo, comería en el restaurante.

_____

d Si comiera en el restaurante, probaría las tapas.

_____

e Si probara las tapas, me gustarían mucho.

_____

f Si me gustaran, estaría contenta.

_____

4 Utiliza la actividad 3 como ejemplo. Utiliza el imperfecto del subjuntivo y el condicional. Escribe cinco frases más para explorar esta posibilidad:

Si tuviera la oportunidad, viviría en España …

_____

_____

_____

_____

_____

1 Lee y subraya los verbos en el pluscuamperfecto del subjuntivo.

Mi madre siempre dice que si no fuera por los esfuerzos de los representantes de los sindicatos, mi abuelo no hubiera salido de la cárcel. Hubiera pasado el resto de su vida como prisionero si no hubieran sacado a la luz su caso. Es dudoso que mi abuela hubiera podido seguir su lucha si fuera la única en protestar.

> ☑ **Consejo**
>
> Sentences with *si hubiera* are often followed by the conditional perfect.
> *Si hubiera ido, habría ganado.* (If I had gone, I would have won.)
> Or by another verb in the pluperfect subjunctive.
> *Si hubiera perdido, hubiera llorado.* (If I had lost, I would have cried.)

> 🔧 **Gramática**
>
> The pluperfect subjunctive is used to talk about what 'would have happened'. It is formed with the imperfect subjunctive of the auxiliary verb *haber* plus the past participle.
>
> *hubiera ido* (I would have gone)
>
> *hubiéramos comido* (we would have eaten)
>
> The imperfect subjunctive of *haber* is:
>
> | | |
> |---|---|
> | hubiera | hubiéramos |
> | hubieras | hubierais |
> | hubiera | hubieran |

2 Empareja las dos mitades de las frases, luego traduce al inglés las frases que has hecho.

a   Si el país hubiera tenido un rey fuerte,

b   Si mi abuela no se hubiera casado con mi abuelo,

c   Si hubiéramos sabido,

d   Si hubieran ganado el partido,

e   Si no fuera por la lluvia,

f   Si hubieras llamado,

i   habríamos pasado unas vacaciones perfectas.

ii   no hubiéramos comprado ese caballo.

iii   no habría habido una guerra.

iv   no te habría estado esperando.

v   habrían ganado la liga.

vi   yo no habría nacido.

_____

_____

_____

_____

_____

_____

⭐ 3 Lee estas frases a–d sobre el fracaso del golpe de estado del 23 de febrero de 1981 en España. Después traduce las frases al inglés.

Ejemplo: Guillermo Quintana dijo que si el rey le hubiera ordenado asaltar las cortes, las hubiera asaltado.

a   Si el rey no hubiera llamado a los capitanes generales, hubieran sacado los tanques a las calles de Madrid.

b   Si el General Armada hubiera estado en el palacio, habría apoyado el golpe.

c   Si hubieran castigado a Tejero después de la Operación Galaxia, no hubiera podido participar en el golpe.

d   Si el ejército hubiera esperado, el gobierno hubiera caído.

a   _____

_____

b   _____

_____

_____

c   _____

_____

d   _____

_____

⚡ Gramática

Sentences with 'if' in the present tense can be followed by:

The future

Si llueve iré a un museo. (If it rains I will go to a museum.)

The present

Si llueve visitamos un museo. (If it rains we visit a museum.)

An imperative

Si llueve, visita un museo. (If it rains, visit a museum.)

1 Completa las frases de tres formas diferentes.

a Si ganas las elecciones … (*formar un gobierno*)

_____

_____

_____

b Si sabes que las noticias son falsas … (*escribir una carta al editor*)

_____

_____

_____

2 Empareja las dos mitades de estas frases. Luego traduce las frases que has hecho.

a Si no ayudamos   **i** los niños morirán.

b Si no ayudáramos   **ii** los niños hubieran muerto.

c Si no hubiéramos ayudado   **iii** los niños morirían.

_____

_____

_____

d Si el rey no actuara   **iv** la democracia hubiera caído.

e Si el rey no hubiera intervenido   **v** la democracia cae.

f Si el rey no hace nada   **vi** la democracia caería.

_____

_____

_____

⚡ Gramática

A sentence with 'if' and the imperfect subjunctive is followed by the conditional.

Si tuviera el tiempo, leería más libros. (If he had the time he would read more books.)

Sentences with 'if' and the pluperfect subjunctive are followed by the conditional perfect or another pluperfect subjunctive:

Si hubiera sabido, no habría ido.

Si hubiera sabido, no hubiera ido.

(If I had known, I wouldn't have gone.)

3 Hay cinco frases con *si*. En cada caso identifica los tiempos verbales.

ª <u>Si</u> vas a una discoteca, se supone que es para bailar. Pero muchas veces ᵇ <u>si</u> van algunos chicos, no bailan sino que se pasan el tiempo bebiendo y charlando. Aunque ᶜ <u>si</u> vas a una disco e intentas hablar, lo encontrarás bastante difícil a causa del ruido. Así que ᵈ <u>si</u> vas a ir, ¡ponte a bailar! Piensa, ᵉ <u>si</u> hubieras bailado, ¿no te hubieras divertido más?

i present + future   **a** _____

ii present + imperative   **b** _____

iii present + present   **c** _____

iv pluperfect subjunctive + pluperfect subjunctive   **d** _____

        e _____

Gramática

In the pronunciation of any Spanish word, one syllable is stressed. This is called the *sílaba tónica*.

When a word ends in a vowel the stress falls on the penultimate vowel.

*ca*sa   *pi*so   *e*rizo   *vi*ve

Words ending in -*n* or -*s* also have the stress on the penultimate vowel.

*ca*sas   *pi*sos   *e*rizos   *vi*ven

Words ending in a consonant (other than -*n* or -*s*) have the stress on the final syllable.

*ho*te**l**   *ha*bla**r**   *vi*va**z**

Where the stress falls on another syllable, a written accent is needed.

*esta*ci**ó**n   *pé*rdida   *Má*laga

---

1 Subraya la sílaba tónica.

a   examen

b   exámenes

c   organización

d   organizaciones

e   jardín

f   jardines

g   iré

h   iremos

i   juego

j   jugamos

k   siete

l   setenta

---

2 Explica en inglés cuando se requiere un acento escrito y por qué.

a   joven, jóvenes

_____

b   jugará, jugaremos

_____

c   obligación, obligaciones

_____

d   público, publico, publicó

_____

✔ Consejo

Accents can also be used to differentiate between words which sound the same but have a different meaning.

hacia / hacía

si / sí

que / qué

---

3 Corrige los errores de cada frase.

a   Los jovenes querian que las autoridádes cambiarán las fechas de los examenes.

_____

b   Habia unos arboles en el jardin publico qué habían sido plantados.

_____

c   Sí quereis, podeis mostrarselas una vez mas.

_____

d   Pondrémos unos numeros telefonicos para memorizar.

_____

e   Es mí teléfono movil. Damelo.

_____

f   ¿Donde esta mi papa?

_____

1 Identifica y corrige las siete frases que contienen errores.

> ☑ **Consejo**
>
> Look back at the pages in this section and think about what errors to look out for.

a Mis padres me quieren ser dentista.

b España hubiera sido un país muy diferente.

c Cuando llega, dile que me llame.

d Después de llegar, fue directo al despacho del rey.

e Si lloviera, los niños van al aula.

f Lo hice para ayudarte.

g La policía detuvo al sospechoso para que él no provocar violencia.

h No quería los niños morir.

i Fue muy peligroso que dejaron a Tejero en libertad.

j Hubiera matara a los diputados comunistas.

2 Imagina lo que hubiera podido pasar el 23 de febrero 1981. Cambia este texto al pluscuamperfecto del subjuntivo.

> ☑ **Consejo**
>
> Check page 24 for irregular past participles.

El rey apoyó el golpe así que llamó a los capitanes generales para decirles que asaltaran las Cortes. Los capitanes generales sacaron los tanques a las calles. La democracia cayó. Se impuso un gobierno militar.

Si el rey hubiera apoyado el golpe,

3 Completa estas frases con tus propias ideas.

Ejemplo: *Si quisiera reducir la pobreza… trabajaría de voluntario.*

a Si pudiera generar dinero para obras caritativas, _____

b Si fuera más fácil encontrar trabajo en España, _____

c Si yo fuera inmigrante en España, _____

d Si no encontrara trabajo, _____

e Si viera a alguien que necesitara ayuda, _____

f Si todos tuviéramos suficiente dinero, _____

4 Traduce las frases al inglés.

a ¿Quién hubiera imaginado que una mujer de cuarenta años y madre de dos hijos quisiera lidiar una corrida de toros?

_____

_____

b Si no fuera por una causa benéfica, sería increíble.

_____

c Si no fuera mujer, ¿nos sorprendería tanto?

_____

d ¿Cómo se pueden reivindicar los derechos de las mujeres, ignorando los derechos de los animales?

_____

_____

5 Escoge la forma correcta del verbo en cada caso.

a Era inevitable que mucha gente **quisiera** / **quieren** / **quería** disuadir a Cristina Sánchez.

b No querían que **lidiará** / **lidia** / **lidiara**.

c A sus hijos no les asustó que su madre **volver** / **volviera** / **volvían** a la plaza de toros.

d Si su esposo hubiera decidido, nunca lo **habría** / **había** / **habré** hecho.

e A sus hijos, les ilusionó mucho que su madre **fuera** / **era** / **iba** torera.

f Eso fue lo que más influyó para que lo **hiciera** / **hicieron** / **hacer**.

6 Traduce al inglés.

Cristina Sánchez ha decidido volver a torear una vez más. Quiere recaudar dinero para la Fundación del doctor Luis Madero que ayuda a los niños que padecen del cáncer. Mucha gente quiso convencerla de que no lo hiciera. Su marido sugirió preguntar a sus hijos, pensando que les asustaría tanto que dirían que no. Pero quedaron muy ilusionados con la propuesta y eso fue el factor determinante.

_____

_____

_____

_____

_____

_____

_____

7 Tapa el texto original de la actividad 6, y traduce tu párrafo al español.

_____

_____

_____

_____

_____

_____

_____

8 Lee y decide cuál de las palabras subrayadas es la correcta en cada caso.

Una cena de jubilados **organizada** / **organizados** por el Ayuntamiento suscitó escándalo en la prensa. Como parte de un espectáculo **después** / **después de** la cena, una bailadora se desnudó de cintura para arriba, **tapandose** / **tapándose** solamente con unas plumas. **Algún** / **Algunas** personas se levantaron de la mesa y se fueron. El alcalde asegura que fue **el** / **él** mismo quien había **contratado** / **contratada** a la vedete. Dice que siempre han **traído** / **trajeron** artistas de ese tipo para entretener a los ancianos. Un portavoz del partido opositor **dije** / **dijo**, "Lo que criticamos es que **se paga** / **se pague** con dinero público".

9 Completa la traducción.

a *I worry about what would happen if I were not able to help.*

Me preocupa lo que _____ si no _____ ayudar. (*pasar, poder*)

b *Think about what you could do if you decided to help.*

Piensa en lo que _____ hacer si _____ ayudar. (*poder, decidir*)

c *If you had to leave your country, where would you go?*

Si _____ que abandonar tu país, ¿adónde

_____? (*tener, ir*)

d *If you chose one Spanish dish, it would have to be tortilla.*

Si _____ un plato español, _____ que ser tortilla. (*escoger, tener*)

e *I know what would happen if you were to ignore the problem.*

Sé lo que _____ si _____ el problema. (*ocurrir, ignorar*)

f *They would like it if you were to come.*

_____ si _____. (*gustar, venir*)

10 Traduce al español.

a When they have finished the airport, will they have any passengers?

_____

_____

b As soon as the minister arrives, they will start to shout.

_____

_____

c After he leaves, they will speak to the press.

_____

_____

d Until he changes his mind, we will carry on protesting.

_____

_____

e When he goes to Spain he always flies.

_____

_____

> ✅ **Consejo**
>
> See page 69 for the subjunctive of futurity.

11 **Traduce al español.**

a I thought it was dangerous.

_____

b He wanted us to help them.

_____

c I didn't think it was too bad.

_____

d They wanted him to change his mind.

_____

e It was impossible for you to do anything about it.

_____

f Young people weren't interested in changing anything.

_____

g Young people wanted to change the world.

_____

12 **Lee las frases y explica el uso de la gramática en cada caso.**

Ejemplo: Fue mi primer cumpleaños.

'Fue' is the preterite of ser and ir. Here it means 'it was'. 'Primer' is the shortened form of 'primero' in front of a masculine singular noun.

a El agua estaba fría.

_____

_____

b El policía quiso abrir la puerta.

_____

_____

c Antes de que sea demasiado tarde, háblele.

_____

_____

d Había vuelto a llover.

_____

_____

e Si no tuvieras otra opción, tampoco podrías aguantar.

_____

_____

f Sus padres se habían conocido antes de la guerra.

_____

_____

13 **Traduce al inglés.**

a El presidente hubiera podido controlar las fuerzas armadas.

_____

b Es un escándalo que hayan negado que la matanza ocurriera.

_____

c Si no fuera por el coraje del obispo, nadie hubiera sabido nada de lo ocurrido.

_____

d Es aún más chocante que fuera asesinado.

_____

1 Empareja las palabras con sus posibles traducciones.

a generar

b dinero

c lanzar

d ganar

e establecer

f una fundación

g fondos

h recaudar

i una organización benéfica

j conseguir

i to raise (money)

ii money

iii to set up

iv a charity

v to make (money)

2 Lee estos sinónimos. Busca diferentes formas de traducirlos al inglés.

a una fundación caritativa / una organización benéfica / una entidad de bien público

_____ / _____ / _____

b generar fondos / recaudar capitales / conseguir dinero

_____ / _____ / _____

3 Traduce al inglés.

a Se ha establecido una fundación que recauda fondos para apoyar a causas benéficas.

_____

_____

b Esa organización ha conseguido un total de trescientos mil euros en un espacio de tres meses.

_____

_____

c La cantidad de dinero generado es mucho más de lo esperado cuando se lanzó la entidad de bien público.

_____

_____

> ✅ **Consejo**
>
> A typical feature of Spanish journalistic style is to use synonyms to avoid repeating a word. Try to replicate this in your translation, but not at the cost of sounding unnatural in English.

4 Empareja la palabra española con su definición en inglés. Luego escribe cuál sería su traducción inglesa.

a When someone is above prosecution.

b A pre-existing right or power.

c Money paid to make up for damages.

d When someone has something taken away.

e A legal entitlement.

i derecho

ii inviolabilidad

iii privar

iv prerrogativa

v indemnizaciones

> ✅ **Consejo**
>
> Don't be put off by legal terms. Work out what it means from the context and find the best English word. Do not invent English words to try to fit the Spanish.

5 Traduce al inglés.

Hablar dos o tres idiomas es de lo más normal. <u>En muchas regiones de España no sorprende que los jóvenes, además de aprender dos idiomas extranjeros hablen o bien en el instituto o bien en casa, otro idioma autonómico y cooficial con el castellano</u>. A veces se trata del idioma materno en niños ya bilingües pero para un porcentaje bastante importante, ir a la escuela implica estudiar en otro idioma. Imagina aprender álgebra en un idioma que estás aprendiendo.

_____

_____

_____

_____

_____

_____

✅ Consejo

You may need to rearrange the underlined sentence to make it work in English. Translate it following the Spanish word order first. Don't miss any words out when you reorder it. Perhaps add a small relative clause with 'which'.

6 Traduce al inglés.

David Ortiz es un jugador de béisbol nacido en la República Dominicana. Su apodo es Big Papi. Ha establecido una fundación que recauda fondos para ayudar a niños que necesitan operarse del corazón. Utiliza sus contactos en el mundo del deporte para organizar torneos de golf que generan dinero para su organización benéfica. En 2008 lanzó una marca de vino con su imagen que consiguió ciento cincuenta mil dólares.

_____

_____

_____

_____

_____

_____

✅ Consejo

Avoid repeating the same words in English when the Spanish uses synonyms. But don't translate literally when it's not good English.

7 Traduce al inglés.

El rey es inviolable, pero bajo la ley nadie puede ser privado de sus derechos aun si otro tuviera prerrogativas. En el caso poco probable de que el rey cometiera un delito, el juez debería investigar los hechos. En esta etapa del proceso legal, la inviolabilidad del rey no tendría efecto ninguno. A partir del momento en que se comprobara la responsabilidad del rey, nadie podría actuar contra él. Pero no significa que pudiera evitar la responsabilidad ni el pago de indemnizaciones establecidos por el juez. Parece increíble que este caso sea posible, pero así lo prevé la Constitución.

_____

_____

_____

_____

_____

_____

_____

1 Escribe la palabra que falta en la traducción. Cuidado con las mayúsculas.

a *My parents used to live in Madrid.*

Mis padres vivían en _____.

b *People from Madrid are called Madrileños.*

Los que vienen de Madrid se llaman

_____.

c *Supporters of Real Madrid are called Madridistas.*

Los hinchas de Real Madrid se llaman

_____.

d *My friends learned Spanish.*

Mis amigos aprendieron el _____.

e *Galicia is in the Northwest of Spain.*

Galicia está en el _____ de España.

f *People from Galicia are Gallegos.*

La gente de Galicia _____ gallegos.

g *The adjective Basque is Vasco, but the language can be called Vascuence.*

El adjetivo es vasco, pero se puede llamar el

_____ vascuence.

2 Escoge la palabra correcta para completar la traducción.

a *They saw me.*

_____ vieron.

b *They came towards me.*

Vinieron hacia _____.

c *It is my family.*

Es _____ familia.

d *He went in front of my parents.*

Fue por delante de _____ padres.

e *They went with me.*

Fueron _____.

f *He told me.*

Me lo dijo a _____.

| conmigo | mí | me | mis | mi |

3 Traduce al español utilizando el imperfecto del subjuntivo y el condicional.

a If I had the money I would go to Spain.

_____

b If we had the opportunity we would help others.

_____

c If I had the time, I would do voluntary work.

_____

d If he committed a crime, he would be arrested.

_____

e If it were the case, it would be unacceptable.

_____

f It would be much better if it were possible.

_____

g If the poor didn't give them food, the rich would have to eat money.

_____

4 Traduce al español.

The language we call 'Spanish' is also called 'Castilian' to differentiate it from the other languages which are spoken in Spain. The other languages are also official languages in their individual Autonomous Communities. Galician and Catalan are not considered to be dialects; they are languages derived, with the passing of time, from Latin. Euskera or Basque is a language of unknown origin, completely different from any other existing European language.

_____

_____

_____

_____

_____

_____

✅ **Consejo**

The texts on page 81 may give you some support with translating these texts.

✅ **Consejo**

Be careful with capital letters.

✅ **Consejo**

Now go back and check all nouns and adjectives for gender, especially any words for languages.

5 Traduce al español.

Every time I see the children we have helped, and I see them coming running towards me, to hug me and say thank you to me, I forget fame and money, and I think of my own children. I think of what would become of me if I were to face the same situation with a child like that and if I didn't have the opportunity to be able to do anything for him. That is what motivates me to do it.

_____

_____

_____

_____

_____

_____

✅ **Consejo**

Use the imperfect subjunctive and then the conditional for hypothetical statements.

If you were to … you would …

6 Traduce al español.

Imagine if the King committed a crime, would he be prosecuted? The question is strange but the answer is quite clear. The King has immunity from prosecution. I have discussed it with colleagues and we have arrived at the conclusion that the Spanish legal bodies would not be able to act, although in the case of some crimes identified by the International Criminal Court, a case could be opened. You would have to find one lawyer in a million to come across a different opinion.

_____

_____

_____

_____

_____

_____

_____

Verb tables

	Present	Preterite	Imperfect	Future	Conditional	Subjunctive
Regular verbs						
-ar **comprar** *to buy* comprando comprado	compro compras compra compramos compráis compran	compré compraste compró compramos comprasteis compraron	compraba comprabas compraba comprábamos comprabais compraban	compraré comprarás comprará compraremos compraréis comprarán	compraría comprarías compraría compraríamos compraríais comprarían	compre compres compre compremos compréis compren
-er **comer** *to eat* comiendo comido	como comes come comemos coméis comen	comí comiste comió comimos comisteis comieron	comía comías comía comíamos comíais comían	comeré comerás comerá comeremos comeréis comerán	comería comerías comería comeríamos comeríais comerían	coma comas coma comamos comáis coman
-ir **subir** *to go up* subiendo subido	subo subes sube subimos subís suben	subí subiste subió subimos subisteis subieron	subía subías subía subíamos subíais subían	subiré subirás subirá subiremos subiréis subirán	subiría subirías subirías subiríamos subiríais subirían	suba subas suba subamos subáis suban
Irregular verbs						
andar *to walk* andando andado	ando andas anda andamos andáis andan	anduve anduviste anduvo anduvimos anduvisteis anduvieron	andaba andabas andaba andábamos andabais andaban	andaré andarás andará andaremos andaréis andarán	andaría andarías andaría andaríamos andaríais andarían	ande andes ande andemos andéis anden
caber *to fit* cabiendo cabido	quepo cabes cabe cabemos cabéis caben	cupe cupiste cupo cupimos cupisteis cupieron	cabía cabías cabía cabíamos cabíais cabían	cabré cabrás cabrá cabremos cabréis cabrán	cabría cabrías cabría cabríamos cabríais cabrían	quepa quepas quepa quepamos quepáis quepan
caer *to fall* cayendo caído	caigo caes cae caemos caéis caen	caí caíste cayó caímos caísteis cayeron	caía caías caía caíamos caíais caían	caeré caerás caerá caeremos caeréis caerán	caería caerías caería caeríamos caeríais caerían	caiga caigas caiga caigamos caigáis caigan
dar *to give* dando dado	doy das da damos dais dan	di diste dio dimos disteis dieron	daba dabas daba dábamos dabais daban	daré darás dará daremos daréis darán	daría darías daría daríamos daríais darían	dé des dé demos deis den
decir *to say* diciendo dicho	digo dices dice decimos decís dicen	dije dijiste dijo dijimos dijisteis dijeron	decía decías decía decíamos decíais decían	diré dirás dirá diremos diréis dirán	diría dirías diría diríamos diríais dirían	diga digas diga digamos digáis digan

	Present	Preterite	Imperfect	Future	Conditional	Subjunctive
estar *to be* estando estado	estoy estás está estamos estáis están	estuve estuviste estuvo estuvimos estuvisteis estuvieron	estaba estabas estaba estábamos estabais estaban	estaré estarás estará estaremos estaréis estarán	estaría estarías estaría estaríamos estaríais estarían	esté estés esté estemos estéis estén
haber *to have* (auxiliary) habiendo habido	he has ha hemos habéis han	hube hubiste hubo hubimos hubisteis hubieron	había habías había habíamos habíais habían	habré habrás habrá habremos habréis habrán	habría habrías habría habríamos habríais habrían	haya hayas haya hayamos hayáis hayan
hacer *to do, make* haciendo hecho	hago haces hace hacemos hacéis hacen	hice hiciste hizo hicimos hicisteis hicieron	hacía hacías hacía hacíamos hacíais hacían	haré harás hará haremos haréis harán	haría harías haría haríamos haríais harían	haga hagas haga hagamos hagáis hagan
ir *to go* yendo ido	voy vas va vamos vais van	fui fuiste fue fuimos fuisteis fueron	iba ibas iba íbamos ibais iban	iré irás irá iremos iréis irán	iría irías iría iríamos iríais irían	vaya vayas vaya vayamos vayáis vayan
poder *to be able* pudiendo podido	puedo puedes puede podemos podéis pueden	pude pudiste pudo pudimos pudisteis pudieron	podía podías podía podíamos podíais podían	podré podrás podrá podremos podréis podrán	podría podrías podría podríamos podríais podrían	pueda puedas pueda podamos podáis puedan
poner *to put* poniendo puesto	pongo pones pone ponemos ponéis ponen	puse pusiste puso pusimos pusisteis pusieron	ponía ponías ponía poníamos poníais ponían	pondré pondrás pondrá pondremos pondréis pondrán	pondría pondrías pondría pondríamos pondríais pondrían	ponga pongas ponga pongamos pongáis pongan
querer *to want* queriendo querido	quiero quieres quiere queremos queréis quieren	quise quisiste quiso quisimos quisisteis quisieron	quería querías quería queríamos queríais querían	querré querrás querrá querremos querréis querrán	querría querrías querría querríamos querríais querrían	quiera quieras quiera queramos queráis quieran
reír *to laugh* riendo reído	río ríes ríe reímos reís ríen	reí reíste rio reímos reísteis rieron	reía reías reía reíamos reíais reían	reiré reirás reirá reiremos reiréis reirán	reiría reirías reirías reiríamos reiríais reirían	ría rías ría riamos riais rían

	Present	**Preterite**	**Imperfect**	**Future**	**Conditional**	**Subjunctive**
saber *to know* sabiendo sabido	sé sabes sabe sabemos sabéis saben	supe supiste supo supimos supisteis supieron	sabía sabías sabía sabíamos sabíais sabían	sabré sabrás sabrá sabremos sabréis sabrán	sabría sabrías sabría sabríamos sabríais sabrían	sepa sepas sepa sepamos sepáis sepan
salir *to leave* saliendo salido	salgo sales sale salimos salís salen	salí saliste salió salimos salisteis salieron	salía salías salía salíamos salíais salían	saldré saldrás saldrá saldremos saldréis saldrán	saldría saldrías saldría saldríamos saldríais saldrían	salga salgas salga salgamos salgáis salgan
ser *to be* siendo sido	soy eres es somos sois son	fui fuiste fue fuimos fuisteis fueron	era eras era éramos erais eran	seré serás será seremos seréis serán	sería serías sería seríamos seríais serían	sea seas sea seamos seáis sean
tener *to have* teniendo tenido	tengo tienes tiene tenemos tenéis tienen	tuve tuviste tuvo tuvimos tuvisteis tuvieron	tenía tenías tenía teníamos teníais tenían	tendré tendrás tendrá tendremos tendréis tendrán	tendría tendrías tendría tendríamos tendríais tendrían	tenga tengas tenga tengamos tengáis tengan
traer *to bring* trayendo traído	traigo traes trae traemos traéis traen	traje trajiste trajo trajimos trajisteis trajeron	traía traías traía traíamos traíais traían	traeré traerás traerá traeremos traeréis traerán	traería traerías traería traeríamos traeríais traerían	traiga traigas traiga traigamos traigáis traigan
valer *to be worth* valiendo valido	valgo vales vale valemos valéis valen	valí valiste valió valimos valisteis valieron	valía valías valía valíamos valíais valían	valdré valdrás valdrá valdremos valdréis valdrán	valdría valdrías valdría valdríamos valdríais valdrían	valga valgas valga valgamos valgáis valgan
venir *to come* viniendo venido	vengo vienes viene venimos venís vienen	vine viniste vino vinimos vinisteis vinieron	venía venías venía veníamos veníais venían	vendré vendrás vendrá vendremos vendréis vendrán	vendría vendrías vendría vendríamos vendríais vendrían	venga vengas venga vengamos vengáis vengan
ver *to see* viendo visto	veo ves ve vemos veis ven	vi viste vio vimos visteis vieron	veía veías veía veíamos veíais veían	veré verás verá veremos veréis verán	vería verías vería veríamos veríais verían	vea veas vea veamos veáis vean

Transition

Nouns (page 5)

1
a iii, **b** x, **c** v, **d** ii, **e** ix, **f** viii, **g** vi, **h** xi

2
m: tema, túnel, paisaje, socialista
f: nacionalidad, intenciones, foto, socialista

3
a hoteles, **b** preocupaciones, **c** ingleses, **d** sistemas, **e** cuartos de baño

4
un problema, la gente va, hoteles, España, la naturaleza, las ciudades, del mar, vacaciones

5
a españoles, **b** ropa, **c** zapatos, **d** la foto, **e** modelo, **f** periodista, **g** una organización

Adjectives (page 6)

1
a change -o to -a, **b** does not change, **c** add an -a, **d** take the accent off the vowel and add an -a, **e** add an -s, **f** add -es, **g** change to a -c, **h** are invariable

2
a trabajadoras, **b** interesante, **c** difíciles, **d** cariñosos, **e** alemanas, **f** felices, **g** web

3
a españolas, tradicionales
b serios, trabajadores
c moderna, útil, web
d capaces

4
a In **i** *inteligente* is singular so it is just the sister who is intelligent. In **ii** it is the brother and the sister.
b In **i** both teachers are hardworking. In **ii** it is just the art teacher because *trabajador* is singular.

Definite and indefinite articles (page 7)

1
a la, **b** El, **c** Los, **d** el, **e** los, **f** La, **g** del, **h** al

2
a un, **b** unos, **c** un, **d** una, **e** un, **f** una, **g** no word needed

3
a La, **b** un, **c** del, **d** la, **e** un, **f** la, **g** la, **h** una, **i** una, **j** un

4
a familias (escaleras), **b** piso (edificio), **c** edificio (piso), **d** escaleras (familias), **e** ascensores (timbres), **f** puerta / calle, **g** timbres (ascensores), **h** puerta (calle)

Word order (page 8)

1
a Tiene un ordenador muy rápido.
b Vivo en una casa moderna.
c Hay unas vistas preciosas.
d Tiene padres generosos.
e Fui a una fiesta de cumpleaños.

2
a **i** this is my old (former) school, **ii** I went to an old school.
b **i** they are great friends, **ii** he has a tall friend
c **i** I feel sorry for the parents, **ii** the family don't have much money
d **i** it was their only experience, **ii** the experience was unique
e **i** there was only water, **ii** there was pure water

3
a tercero, **b** bueno, **c** alguno, **d** ninguno, **e** malo

4
a Es una ciudad preciosa.
b Es una ciudad muy antigua.
c Es un gran amigo y una buena persona.
d Es un buen amigo y una gran persona.
e Es una gran amiga y una buena persona.
f Es una buena amiga y una gran persona.

The present tense – regular and irregular verbs (page 9)

1

	-ar/-er/-ir?	person?	meaning
vivimos	-ir	1st plural	we live
escribís	-ir	2nd plural	you write (plural)
nada	-ar	3rd singular	he/she/it swims (or *usted*)
estudias	-ar	2nd singular	you study (singular)
escogéis	-er	2nd plural	you choose (plural)
bebemos	-er	1st plural	we drink

2
a We prefer to spend the holidays in England.
b They live in Spain.
c My mother rings me every day.
d You drink too much.
e My brothers decide where we eat.

3
a *nadamos* we swim
b *visito* I visit
c *ayudáis* you help
d *sale* he/she/it goes out
e *pones* you put
f *olvidan* they forget
g *abro* I open
h *hacen* they do/make

4
hago, pongo, digo, vengo, salgo, caigo, traigo, conduzco, padezco, ofrezco, crezco, establezco

The preterite tense – regular verbs (page 10)

1a
they have accents

1b
-ar verbs end in -amos for both, -ir verbs end in -imos for both, -er has emos for present and -imos for past

2
a vi, b iii, c vii, d v, e iv, f ii, g i

3
llegó he arrived, *miraron* they looked at, *entró* he came in, *murmuró* he muttered, *sacó* he took out, *empezó* he started

4
Aquel día llegué tarde al instituto. Los otros alumnos trabajaban en silencio y me miraron asustados cuando entré de repente. 'Lo siento,' murmuré y saqué mis cuadernos y empecé a trabajar.

The imperfect tense (page 11)

1
a My grandparents lived (used to live) in a small town.
b My parents hated (used to hate) living far from the city.
c My dad went (used to go) to school every day.
d My mum helped (used to help) with household chores.

2
a comía, b comía, c hacía, d jugábamos, e trabajaban

3
vivía I lived/used to live, *no me gustaba* I didn't like, *tenía que* I had to, *no estaban* they weren't in, *me permitían* they let me

4
imperfect: we were living, was, used to go out, I had to stay at home, were going to go
preterite: decided, was not happy, did not say
Vivíamos en México y todo era muy diferente. Mi hermano salía a ver a sus amigos, pero yo tenía que quedarme en casa. Un día mis amigos iban a ir al cine y decidí ir también. A mi madre no le pareció bien, pero no le dijo nada a mi papá.

The conditional tense (page 12)

1a
Do not remove the -ar/-er/-ir ending
1b
-er/-ir endings for the imperfect
1c
they are the same endings

2
a we would live
b they would go
c I would get married
d my brother would buy
e you would win/earn

3
saldría, tendría, pondría, diría, vendría, haría, sabría, habría, podría, valdría, querría, cabría

4
a jugaríamos, b tendría, c podría, d gustaría, e saldría

5
Me gustaría vivir en una ciudad. Iría al cine cada día y vería todas las nuevas películas. Iría de compras y compraría ropa preciosa. Invitaría a mis amigos y comeríamos en restaurantes caros. Trabajaría en un banco y ganaría mucho dinero. Mis padres vendrían a vivir cerca.

The future and immediate future tenses (page 13)

1
a Trabajaré en una fábrica.
b Mi hermano será abogado.
c Tendremos una casa en la playa.
d Mis padres vendrán a visitarme.
e Podrás visitarme también.

2
En el futuro las cosas serán diferentes. Tendremos robots para hacer todo el trabajo. Nos harán la vida fácil. Viviremos mil años porque transferirán nuestra personalidad a un disco.

3
a iii, b i, c ii, d iv, e vi, f v

4
En el futuro las cosas van a ser diferentes. Vamos a tener robots para hacer todo el trabajo. Van a hacer fácil nuestra vida. Vamos a vivir mil años porque van a transferir nuestra personalidad a un disco.

Negatives and infinitive constructions (page 14)

1
a iv, b v, c viii, d vi, e iii, f ii, g i, h vii

2
a to feel like, b to have just, c to be about to, d to start to, e to start to, f to help, g to stop, h to do something again

3
a No me gusta nada en esa tienda.
b No tienen buenos precios tampoco.
c No tienen ni buen servicio ni buenos productos.
d Ni siquiera tienen unos empleados informados.
e Nadie te ayuda.
f No voy a volver nunca a comprar cosas allí.

Section 1

The present tense – radical changing verbs (page 15)

1
prefiero
quieren
puedes
requiere
mantienen

2
a tener, b jugar, c volver, d pedir, e venir, f dormir

3
a queremos, b requieren, c mantenemos, d jugamos, e duermo, f preferimos, g vuelve

4

Pasamos mucho tiempo hablando por el teléfono móvil. Jugamos con los videojuegos, escuchamos música y preferimos salir siempre con el teléfono. Lo utilizamos todo el tiempo, por ejemplo si queremos saber algo, lo buscamos en Internet.

5

a juega, **b** marca, **c** pierde, **d** tiene, **e** muerde, **f** representa, **g** suele, **h** podemos, **i** tiene

Reflexive verbs (page 16)

1

a se maquillan

b se afeitan

c me acuesto

d lavarse/lavarme, etc.

2

a se casa/se casó

b acordarnos

c se levantan

d te imaginas

e se divorcian / se divorciaron

3 and 4

nos incluyamos: a

se transforman: d

te inspiras: e

se enfrentaron al: f

nos podemos permitir (permitirse): a

se ha terminado: e

5

El número de españoles que se casa se reduce cada año. Una familia no se define por el matrimonio. Mucha gente convive sin casarse, pero se quieren de todas maneras.

Impersonal verbs (page 17)

1

a iv, **b** i, **c** ii, **d** iii

2

a It interests young people a lot.

b It annoys my parents.

c I loved it.

d It doesn't matter to us.

e I care about you a lot.

f My feet hurt.

3

a A mis padres no les gusta.

b A los jóvenes no les importa.

c Me preocupas.

d Les encanta.

e No nos gustan los tomates.

4 and 5

Los jóvenes piensan que es importante trabajar duro. Les importa tener un buen trabajo y les encanta ganar dinero. Salvar el planeta no les preocupa.

Continuous tenses (page 18)

1

estaba viviendo – I was living, *estaba trabajando* – I was working, *estoy viviendo* – I am living, *estoy ganando* – I am earning

2

a Mi empresa está perdiendo dinero.

b Estoy volviendo a España.

c Estaba trabajando en Marruecos.

d Estoy llegando a mi país.

3

a está viviendo

b estaba trabajando

c está trabajando

d están construyendo

4

Después de trabajar en Marruecos, ahora está viviendo en España. En vez de trabajar en la construcción, está trabajando en la agricultura. Estaba construyendo un pueblo nuevo, y aunque siguen construyendo el pueblo, él no está trabajando allí.

The preterite tense – irregular verbs (1) (page 19)

1

a ix, **b** i, **c** ii, **d** iii, **e** iv, **f** v, **g** vi, **h** vii, **i** viii, **j** x

a I said, **b** he/she/it wanted, **c** he/she/it put, **d** they could, **e** we brought, **f** they did/made, **g** I was, **h** they knew, **i** I came, **j** he/she/it fitted

2

a tuve, **b** hicimos, **c** dijeron, **d** trajo, **e** estuvisteis, **f** pudiste, **g** pusimos, **h** supe

3

vinieron – they came, *hicieron* – they made, *quisieron* – they tried, *no pudieron* – they couldn't, *dijo* – he said

4

Mis tíos no vinieron a mi fiesta. Pudieron mandarme un regalo. Dije que entendía pero no hicieron gran esfuerzo.

Avoiding the passive by using *se* (page 20)

1

a Spanish is spoken here.

b Breakfast is served at seven o'clock.

c No running.

d Glass recycled.

e Wanted, dead or alive.

f For sale.

2

a fútbol

b altavoces

c permiso de conducir

3

a *se juega* – it is played, *se gana* – it is won, *no se puede* – you can't

b *se conectan* – they are connected, *se utilizan* – they are used, *se pueden encontrar* – they can be found

c *se requiere* – it is required, *se consigue* – it is obtained, *se tiene que hacer* – you have to do

4

Se juega con un balón. No se permite tocar el balón con los pies. Se marcan puntos cuando el balón se mete en una cesta. No se puede correr con el balón. Se juega con dos equipos.

Comparatives and superlatives (page 21)

1

a C, **b** S, **c** C, **d** C, **e** S, **f** S

2

a más trabajadora que

b mejor que

c más moderno

3

a el más rápido

b la más cara

c soy el/la mejor

Ser and estar (page 22)

1

Perfil (ser)	Estado (estar)
estudiante	cansado/a
joven	en el instituto
inteligente	preocupado/a
alto/a	
español/a	

2

a profession

b temporary state

c definition

d permanent quality

e position

f present continuous

3

a ser, **b** estamos, **c** están, **d** es

4

a Mis padres son socialistas.

b Mis amigos están en España.

c Eres muy listo pero estás un poco cansado y aburrido.

d Normalmente es muy callado pero hoy está nervioso, por eso habla demasiado.

The perfect tense (page 23)

1

a Ha cambiado.

b Han progresado.

c He decidido.

d Ha disminuido.

e Habéis terminado.

f Hemos inventado.

g Has cambiado.

h Han terminado.

i Han decidido.

j Hemos progresado.

2

a Hernández ha marcado un gol.

b Hernández y Albero han discutido.

c El árbitro ha expulsado a los dos jugadores.

d El Barcelona ha perdido.

e Hemos ganado el partido.

3

hemos experimentado – we have experienced, *Se ha convertido* – It has become, *han cambiado* – have changed, *han tenido que* – they have had to

Irregular past participles (page 24)

1 and 2

a *ver* – seen

b *hacer* – done

c *romper* – broken

d *cubrir* – covered

e *poner* – put

f *decir* – said

g *morir* – died

h *abrir* – open

i *volver* – returned

3

a He visto.

b Hemos roto.

c Ha escrito.

d Han descubierto.

e Ha vuelto.

f Ha muerto.

g Has visto.

h Han dicho.

4

a escrito, **b** vuelto, **c** descubierto, **d** roto, **e** abierto, **f** visto, **g** dicho, **h** hecho, **i** muerto

The conditional and future perfect (page 25)

1 and 2

habrían cambiado – they would have changed, *habríamos salido* – we would have gone out, *habría jugado* – he/she would have played

habrá terminado – he/she will have finished, *habremos decidido* – we will have decided, *habré ido* – I will have gone

3

a habré comido

b habremos salido

c habrán llegado

4

a habría comido

b habría decidido

c habrías cambiado

5

Within ten years we will have discovered new drugs which will have stopped hair from growing. I imagine that hairdressers would have protested but nobody would have listened to them, as they will have become irrelevant. In fact, I think we would have sent the hairdressers to colonise another planet.

The pluperfect tense (page 26)

1 and 2

habíamos ido – we had gone, *habían sido* – they had been, *habíais tenido* – you had had, *te habías enamorado* – you had fallen in love

3

había cometido
habíamos sido
había visto

4

a habíamos llegado
b había llegado
c había tenido
d había dicho
e había decidido

5

Previamente… su ex novio había venido a México a buscarla.
Previamente su ex novio… se había escapado de la cárcel.
Previamente Tracy… se había enamorado del doctor.
Previamente la familia del doctor… había muerto.
Previamente Tracy… había conocido a un doctor.
Previamente Tracy… se había ido a México.
Previamente la policía… le había dado una nueva identidad.
Previamente Tracy… había sido testigo de un crimen.
Previamente Tracy… había tenido un novio.

Mixed practice

Mixed practice (page 27)

1

i a
His cousin had been born a couple of years before.
ii b
Immigration will have ceased to be a problem.
iii a
The members of the group had met in LA.
iv c
By now they would have told you if they needed you.
v b
There won't have been any unnecessary changes.
vi c
Who could have been the most important?

2a

a estoy pensando
b están cambiando
c estás apoyando
d estaban hablando
e estábamos corriendo

2b

a intento
b esperaban
c llueve
d pensaba
e trabajáis

3

requiere – requerir, puede – poder, dice – decir, mueren – morir, quieren – querer, juegan – jugar

4

Flamenco is associated with the region of Andalucia. It is performed at parties and it can also be seen in bars for tourists. People believe it is a type of dance, but in reality it is based on singing and is accompanied by guitar music.

Mixed practice (page 28)

5

a se pasa
b se evita
c se organizan
d se mantienen
e Se celebran, se llaman

6

a vamos/iremos/vamos a ir
b trajeron
c viene
d ha sido
e estoy estudiando
f ganó
g copiaba/estaba copiando

7

presente:
digo – I say
juego – I play
como – I eat
quiere – he/she wants
hago – I do

pretérito:
dije – I said
jugué – I played
comió – he/she ate
quiso – he/she wanted
hizo – he/she did

imperfecto:
decía – I was saying
jugaba – I was playing
comía – I was eating
queríamos – we wanted
hacían – they were doing

futuro:
diré – I will say
jugaré – I will play
comeremos – we will eat
querrán – they will want
hará – he/she will do

participio pasado:
dicho – said
jugado – played
comido – eaten
querido – wanted
hecho – done

Mixed practice (page 29)

8
a I have, present tense first person with *g*, 1st person of *tener*
b they will go out, future tense with irregular stem, 3rd person plural of *salir*
c we were, strong preterite, 1st person plural of *estar*
d I/he/she was running, imperfect tense 1st or 3rd person of *correr*
e he/she has spoken, 3rd person of perfect tense of *hablar*
f we would go, 1st person plural conditional of *ir*
g I/he/she had returned, irregular past participle, 1st or 3rd person of *haber*
h we learn, 1st person plural present tense of *aprender*
i they returned, 3rd person plural preterite of *volver*
j we understood, 1st person plural preterite of *entender*

9
a nos gusta
b piensan
c ha terminado
d fuiste
e he ido / he sido / he estado
f hay
g estoy leyendo / leo
h nos quedamos
i llegaron
j dijimos
k se vistieron

10
a ¿Ha terminado sus deberes?
b Mi hermano llegó el martes.
c Nos duele la cabeza.
d Os veis muy guapos.
e Se irá a Madrid.
f Queremos dormir.
g Mi primo había venido.
h Vivía en Alicante.

Mixed practice (page 30)

11
a están, b está, c es, d ser, e está, f están, g estoy, h es

12
a My younger sister plays better than me.
b My older brother scored more than five goals.
c I didn't score as many goals as him.
d The person who scored most goals was my sister.
e Both my brother and my sister are very good.
f I am the worst in the family.
g The person who works most is me.
h My sister doesn't study as much as my brother.
i My brother and sister are not as hard-working as me.
j The more I work, the more I learn.

13
El rugby se considera bastante peligroso pero mi hermano menor es muy bueno. Juega muy bien y es el mejor de su curso. Entrenaba los fines de semana pero ahora sólo juega en el instituto. Ha jugado con el instituto y ganaron todos los partidos. Jugaría para un club, pero tiene que ir a la casa de mi papá los fines de semana. Va a jugar con Escocia algún día.

Translation practice: Spanish to English (page 31)

1
a He is my favourite artist.
b She is a model.
c He is an actor.
d He is a dancer.
e She is a composer.
f He is a fashion designer.
g She is a very famous author.
h He is a celebrity and very famous.
i The English artist is a rock star. He lives in Spain.

2
a It has been
b He/She is working
c We like
d I brought
e He/She has
f He/She/It will finish
g He/She/It was working/used to work
h It would be

3
a He is one of the best Spanish singers.
b It is the best known building in the city.
c He/She has a less famous brother.
d It would be better/best to spend the whole day there.
e He/She hadn't visited such a pretty city.

4
a It has become very famous.
b It was begun in 1896.
c It is considered a masterpiece.
d It can be visited.
e It is recommended you spend several hours there.

Translation practice: Spanish to English (page 32)

5
Fergie is one of many celebrities with Mexican roots. She has been a dancer, composer, model and fashion designer, but she is best known as an actress and singer. She has collaborated with some of the best rap artists. Today she is pursuing a solo career. Less well known is her charity work, and the fact that her perfume brand has been one of the most successful.

6
Smartphones today allow us to participate in social networks while dinner is being prepared or during a meeting at work. They brought enormous benefits for social life and life at work, but they also have their negative side. Technology changed our habits, and for some people it has become an obsession. It has been calculated that typically we check our mobiles up to a hundred and fifty times a day.

7
It has been calculated that the Basilica of the Sagrada Familia will be completed in the year 2026. It will be a hundred and forty-four years since its construction started. It is the masterpiece of the Catalan architect Gaudí, and the most famous attraction of the city of Barcelona. For the first sixteen years of its construction, Gaudí lived in the cathedral, and today he is buried in the crypt. Its design incorporates the organic style of its creator with the symbolism of the Catholic Church. The original plan had eighteen spires, including one of a hundred and seventy-two metres which would be the tallest church spire in the world.

Translation practice: English to Spanish (page 33)

1

a ii, **b** iii, **c** v, **d** i, **e** iv, **f** vi, **g** vii, **h** ix, **i** viii

2

Best answers following example in activity 1:
a buscó en, **b** comprobó, **c** tomó, **d** monitorizó,
e comprobamos, **f** consultó

3

a iii, **b** iv, **c** ii, **d** i, **e** iii
f ix, **g** v, **h** vii, **i** vi, **j** viii

Translation: English into Spanish (page 34)

4

Taboo es otra estrella del rock con raíces mexicanas. Su
nombre verdadero es Jaime Luis Gomez. Es norteamericano/
estadounidense pero su padre nació en Morelia, la ciudad
más preciosa de México. Es cantante y actor, mejor conocido
como miembro de los Black Eyed Peas. Ha cantado en
español y en inglés. Como artista en solitario, ha grabado una
canción para apoyar a una organización benéfica que lucha
contra el cáncer.

5

El reloj inteligente modifica nuestro estilo de vida. En vez
de monitorizar tu teléfono, tu reloj puede monitorizarte
a ti. Registra tu actividad y te alerta de acontecimientos.
Se venden con la promesa de que traen beneficios para la
salud, pero para muchos se han convertido en una irritación,
por sus constantes recordatorios y noticias. Y ahora puedes
comprar un cepillo de dientes que se comunica con tu móvil,
que se conecta con tu reloj, y que te dice que tienes que
cepillarte los dientes más a menudo.

6

La Catedral de Córdoba se considera como la obra maestra
de la arquitectura de *Al-Andalus*. Es el monumento más
importante de Córdoba y uno de los sitios más visitados de
España. Originalmente se construyó como una mezquita.
Era la segunda mezquita más grande del mundo en
aquella época. La Catedral Católica se construyó en medio
de la mezquita. El arquitecto fue Hernán Ruiz. Cuando
el Emperador Carlos quinto vio el edificio, dijo, 'Habéis
destruido lo que era único al mundo y habéis puesto en su
lugar lo que se ve en todas partes.'

Section 2

Direct object pronouns (page 35)

1

a iii, **b** i, **c** iv, **d** ii

2

a i, **b** iv, **c** ii, **d** iii

3

a La toman muy en serio.
b Los valoramos.
c Tenemos que aceptarlas. / Las tenemos que aceptar.
d Las estaba explorando.
e Lo he dejado.

4

Me interesan mucho las figuras coleccionables de ciencia
ficción. Cuando voy a las tiendas siempre las busco. Por
ejemplo el fin de semana estaba con mis amigos y vi una
figura que necesitaba para mi colección. La compré pero era
muy cara. Mi colección tiene un valor muy elevado pero no
voy a venderla. Voy a seguir coleccionándolas.

Indirect object pronouns (page 36)

1

a Le, **b** Nos, **c** Te, **d** os

2

a I said nothing to him/to her.
b He/She showed the photos to us.
c I am going to give a bicycle to you.
d He/She explained the grammar to them.
e It doesn't matter to me.
f He/She fixed the device for me.

3

a He told a secret to me. *Me dijo un secreto.*
b They sent an email to her. *Le enviaron un correo electrónico.*
c I will give a present to him. *Le voy a dar un regalo.*
d She wrote a poem for him. *Le escribió un poema.*
e They are offering a special price to me. *Me están ofreciendo / Están ofreciéndome un precio especial.*
f They sold the computer to him. *Le vendieron el ordenador.*
g They bought a car for us. *Nos compraron un coche.*

The passive voice (page 37)

1

a iv, **b** i, **c** ii, **d** v, **e** iii

2

a iv, **b** v, **c** vi, **d** i, **e** ii, **f** iii

3

a El ordenado fue vendido a un precio excesivo.
b Un nuevo tipo de ordenador fue inventado.
c Mi portátil ha sido reparado.
d La tableta fue reparada.

4

es utilizada por gran cantidad de profesionales
será reemplazado por nuevos inventos

5

a han sido desarrolladas
b será controlado
c he sido reemplazado/a

The subjunctive (page 38)

1

1 a, f, g
2 b, e, i, j
3 c, d, h

2

a No. It's not wanting someone else to do something.
b Yes. Wanting someone else to do something.
c Yes. Doubt/don't think
d No. I DO think.
e Yes, uses adjective of feeling with *ser*.
f No, statement of fact.

3
nades, vengas, sea, esté, hagas, vayas, hayan

4
-ar verbs take *-er* endings. *-er/-ir* take *-ar* endings.

The present subjunctive (page 39)

1
a poder, **b** ayudar, **c** entender, **d** saber, **e** llegar, **f** ser, **g** venir, **h** decir

2
a I, **b** S, **c** S, **d** I, **e** S, **f** I, **g** S

3
a nademos, **b** corran, **c** hagan, **d** diga, **e** vayan, **f** juguemos, **g** saquen

4
a olvides, **b** saque, **c** sea, **d** expliques, **e** digan, **f** vaya, **g** hagan, **h** podáis

The perfect subjunctive (page 40)

1
Subjunctive: **b d f**
a Not doubt. I DO think…
b Wanting someone else to do something
c Statement of fact not grammatically linked to the value judgement
d Value judgement
e I DO think
f Value judgement

2
a No pienso que los móviles hayan cambiado la vida.
b No es verdad que la familia tradicional haya desaparecido.
c No es mi opinión que la iglesia se haya adaptado a la vida moderna.
d No sé si los españoles hayan cambiado su actitud hacia la monarquía.
e No digo que haya sido muy importante preservar las costumbres regionales.
f No supongo que hayas leído *La Sombra del Viento*.

Demonstrative adjectives and pronouns (page 41)

1
a estas, **b** ese, **c** aquellos, **d** este, **e** esas, **f** esos

2
a Ese, **b** Ese, **c** Eso/Ese (both), **d** Esta, **e** este, **f** aquello

3
There are several kinds of pet and that can present a problem if you want to work with animals. This kind of work requires knowledge and experience. The latter is perhaps the most important thing. For example, between this tortoise and that snake, there is a great difference, but also this dog can have a totally different personality from this other one. That is what makes the job interesting.

Possesssive adjectives and pronouns (page 42)

1
a su, **b** mi, **c** su, **d** nuestros, **e** sus, **f** nuestras

2
a ii, **b** iii, **c** iv, **d** i

3
Me gusta tu idea pero la mía es la mejor. Me gusta la tuya pero no tanto como la mía. Nuestro trabajo es siempre el mejor, y nuestras ideas son fantásticas, normalmente las tuyas pero esta vez la mía.

Indefinite adjectives and pronouns (page 43)

1
a ninguna, **b** todos, **c** Cualquiera, **d** otra, **e** algún, **f** otra, **g** cada, **h** cualquier

2
a He/She has some good ideas.
b He/She doesn't have a single good idea.
c Some are good ideas.
d Some people have good ideas.
e He/She has several ideas.
f He/She has another idea.
g He/She puts forward any old idea.
h He/She explores every possibility.
i He/She explores all the possibilities.
j Everything is possible.

3
a Tiene varias ideas buenas, pero algunas son mejores que otras.
b Tiene pocas ideas buenas, pero no todas son malas.
c Tiene algunas ideas, algunas buenas, otras malas.
d Algunos tienen buenas ideas, algunos tienen malas.
e Otra posibilidad es explorar todas vuestras ideas.
f …luego puedes eliminar algunas pero no todas.
g El problema es cuando no tienes ninguna idea.
h A veces cualquier idea es buena.

The imperative (page 44)

1
a iii, **b** vii, **c** vi, **d** v, **e** viii, **f** iv, **g** ii, **h** i

2
a iv, **b** ii, **c** iii, **d** i

3
a Give me that.
b Do your homework.
c Be quiet.
d Don't put that there.
e Don't believe it.
f Take out your exercise books.

4
a Lee
b Terminad
c Pon
d tires
e Conduzca

Mixed practice

Mixed practice (page 45)

1
c He doesn't think it's necessary.
d We need you to help us with the homework.
e Don't study so much.
g It's a shame that you get bad grades.

2
a seas, b hagas, c haya, d estudie, e sea

3
a Él no piensa que haya cometido una falta.
b No creo que llore.
c Necesita que el entrenador le ayude.
d No quiere que le digan qué hacer.
e Siento que el jefe no quiera/haya querido hablarme.

4
a Mi profesor piensa que es mejor que hagamos nuestros deberes.
b Elena no piensa que sea difícil aprender inglés.
c Tu padre quiere impedir que seas perezoso.
d Es genial que hayas aprendido a hablar español.
e No pienses que no puedas tener éxito.

Mixed practice (page 46)

5
a Los coches son fabricados en Zaragoza.
b El acero es extraído en Asturias.
c Las naranjas son cultivadas en Valencia.
d El país es gobernado desde Madrid.
e La independencia catalana es reivindicada en Barcelona.
f El queso es producido en La Mancha.
g La cerveza es consumida en Inglaterra.
h Aragón es conocido por sus paisajes impresionantes.

6
a esto, b esta, c Este, d estos, e estos, f esto, g Estas, h estos

7
a La golpeó con un palo.
b La llenaron de dulces.
c Las colgamos en el patio.
d Les regalaron dulces.
e Les mandó una tarjeta.
f La mandó a sus amigas.
g Les trajeron regalos.
h Los trajeron para los niños.

Mixed practice (page 47)

8
a bebe, b no corras, c dormid, d piensa, e ayude, f vengan, g no bebas, h no ayudéis, i no diga, j pon

9
a ¡Levantaos!
b ¡No comas!
c ¡Venga!
d ¡Vive!
e ¡Dádmelo!
f ¡Démelo!
g ¡No me lo des!

10
a iii, b i, c ii, d iv, e vii, f v, g vi, h viii

11
a su, b nuestros, c Nuestras, d Vuestros, e cuyas, f las nuestras

Mixed practice (page 48)

12
a Cada, b Algunas, c Cualquier, d Todo, e otro, f Ninguno

13
conozcáis
presentadora
la voz
Primer Impacto
trasmitía
ha ganado
importantes
incluyendo

14
perfect tense: han dejado
present tense radical changing verb: sugiere / empiece
reflexive verb: volverse
present continuous: están empezando
imperfect tense: llevaba
past participle: obligados
subjunctive: empiece

15
a eficaces
b fría
c construir
d vaya
e tendremos/tenemos
f Pon
g gustó
h vengan
i dijo / decía
j primer
k busques (busco)
l es

Translation practice: Spanish to English (page 49)

1
a chapel, b Pope, c chalice, d sin, e disciple, f convent, g monastery, h pilgrim, i miracle

2
a dish, b mud, c role, d earthenware, e box, f paper, g card

3
a Spain is made up of 17 autonomous communities.
b Puebla is the name of a city and also of a Mexican state.
c The countries of England, Scotland, N Ireland and Wales are known as the United Kingdom.
d The King united the nation in the face of the crisis.
e The Christian warriors retook the Iberian Peninsula.
f Under the Catholic Monarchs, Ferdinand and Isabella, the main kingdoms of Spain were brought together.

Translation practice: Spanish to English (page 50)

4

With Christmas comes the tradition of smashing piñatas. The piñata is a pot made of earthenware or cardboard which is covered in coloured paper. It contains sweets, toys and fruit. The piñata is hung up and then you take turns to hit it with a stick. There are different designs of them, from donkeys to ninja turtles. But the Christmas piñata has seven points to represent the seven mortal sins.

5

The food of the state of Puebla is recognised not only nationally but internationally for the variety of its dishes. They are recipes full of tastes, smells and colours. With their origin in the kitchens of convents or private homes, they have come to be spread all over the country. The best example is *mole poblano* with more than twenty ingredients. It is one of (many) gastronomic things to be proud of from Puebla.

6

The Holy Grail is to be found in a chapel of Valencia Cathedral. It is a stone chalice which dates from the first century. The legend tells that after Christ's death, his few belongings were shared out between his disciples. According to the story, Saint Peter, the first Pope, took the chalice to Rome. In the Middle Ages a Spanish Pope took it to Huesca in Aragón. In turn, a King of Aragón handed it over to the Cathedral. It is an important witness to the continuity of Christianity in the peninsula, linking the development of different Christian kingdoms with the power of the Church, and its role in the creation of a united nation, made up of different autonomous communities.

Translation: English to Spanish (page 51)

1

a entregué, b regalé, c conferir, d donó

2

a hasta, b hasta que, c después de, d a causa de, e después de que

3

a Dejó su país.
b Dejó de fumar.
c Se quedó con todo el dinero.
d No le dejaron ir.

4

a guiso, b azafrán, c habichuelas/alubias, d fideos, e caldo

Translation: English to Spanish (page 52)

5

Un aguinaldo es una pequeña bolsa de fruta o dulces que se regala en Navidad en México. Se regalan/Son regalados a cada invitado con ocasión de 'posadas' que es cuando los amigos y la familia representan la llegada de la sagrada familia en busca de dónde hospedarse. Cantan y llaman a distintas casas buscando una habitación. En la última casa a la que llegan, se encienden las luces y todos festejan.

6

Los arroces son de gran importancia en la identidad nacional y regional españolas. Hay tres tipos básicos. El arroz caldoso se sirve como una sopa. El arroz meloso tiene menos líquido, pero el arroz se cuece hasta que esté blando y untuoso. La paella se cuece hasta que el arroz esté 'seco' y no quede nada de caldo. En Cataluña el plato 'fideuá' es parecido pero se hace con fideos en vez de arroz.

7

El monasterio de San Juan de la Peña es uno de los monumentos de la Edad Media más importantes de España. Se asocia / Es asociado a la leyenda del nacimiento del reino cristiano de Aragón y el comienzo de la Reconquista de España. Los guerreros se reunieron allí para escoger a su caudillo antes de la batalla en la que una cruz en llamas apareció de manera milagrosa en el cielo. Muchos de los reyes de Aragón están sepultados/enterrados en una capilla que hay allí. Está situado en una posición espectacular debajo de una enorme piedra, y se extiende dentro de una cueva. Durante muchos años el Santo Grial se guardaba allí para atraer a los peregrinos.

Section 3

The present tense (page 53)

1
a son, b vas, c es, d Hemos, e están, f vamos, g está

2
a Vamos a España cada año.
b Hemos comprado una casa en Santander.
c Está cerca del mar.
d Es bastante pequeña.
e Mis padres van allí en el invierno.
f Están allí ahora.

3
ha, es, ha, hemos, son, vas, estás, son

4
Las tapas son típicas de la gastronomía española. Si vas a un bar puedes pedir una ración o una tapa. Si vais todos a compartir, es mejor pedir una ración. Así que si estás en España y nunca has probado las tapas, es una experiencia que recomiendo.

The preterite and imperfect tenses (page 54)

1
preterite: dio, decidió, empezó, fue, dejó, pasó, ayudaron
imperfect: trabajaba, comía, corría, estaba, comía, dormía, veía, jugaba, hacían

2
used to eat – I
changed – P
they used to eat – I
they started – P
used to eat – I
the diet changed – P
they found themselves – P

3
a comían, b cambió, c comían, d se pusieron, e empezaron, f comían, g cambió, h se encontraron

4
a eran, b vivían, c iban, d ayudaban, e iban

The preterite tense – radical changing/irregular verbs (2) (page 55)

1
a morir, b conferir, c reñir, d sentir, e pedir, f dormir, g sonreír

2
dormir

dormí	dormimos
dormiste	dormisteis
durmió	durmieron

3
a Me dio miedo.
b Nos dimos prisa.
c No me dieron tiempo.
d Fuimos a casa.
e Fue un desastre.

4
a Pedimos la cuenta.
b Pidió ayuda.
c Nos dimos cuenta.
d Fue mi hermano.
e Durmieron.
f Dormí.
g No me di cuenta.

5
a durmió, dio
b riñeron, murió
c sintió
d fueron
e fue, riñó
f nos reímos

Compound tenses (page 56)

1
a I have been, b They are playing, c They have danced, d I am enjoying, e I have learned

2
a subido, b buscando, c han, d está, e Ha

3
you will have been visiting, we had been spending, had been listening, we had been sharing, after having been enjoying

4
a He estado tocando la guitarra.
b Habrá estado cantando.
c Habríamos estado escuchando.
d Habían estado bailando.

Direct and indirect object pronouns (page 57)

1
a I: Nos, D: lo
b I: me, D: la
c I: Me, D: la
d I: te, D: lo

2
a Me los vendieron.
b Me lo dedicó.
c Te lo explicará.

3
a se la, b se los, c se lo, d se las

4
a Tiene unas canciones fabulosas. Me las cantó.
b Me gustan sus poemas. Nos los leyó.
c Tenía una pregunta. Así que se la pregunté.
d Necesitaba una foto. Me la sacó.
e Te gusta el DVD. Te lo compraré.
f Me gusta el DVD. Cómpramelo.

Adverbs (page 58)

1
a cuidadosa, cuidadosamente
b peligrosa, peligrosamente
c especial, especialmente
d natural, naturalmente
e simpática, simpáticamente
f afortunada, afortunadamente
g desalentadora, desalentadoramente

2
tranquilamente, paulatinamente, claramente, consistentemente
paulatinamente – paso a paso
claramente – claro
consistentemente – de forma consistente

3
Adjetivos: natural, gran, demasiada, subterránea, irreparables
Adverbios: rápidamente, inmediatamente, demasiado

4
El efecto de la extracción constante de agua está mal interpretado, pero inevitablemente reseca la reserva natural.

Prepositions (page 59)

1
a at/to b in/on c of/from d with e without f towards g from h until i under j inside k on top of l above m between n next to o after

2
a I went on foot.
b I was standing up.
c I made it by hand.
d He did it his way.
e I was thinking of you.
f I dreamed of my grandma last night.

3
a iv, b ii, c iii, d v, e vi, f i

4
a I was going to buy a present for my niece.
b As I was driving down the road the car in front broke down.
c Unluckily we crashed.
d Obviously, it was just an accident.
e At least nobody was hurt.
f I couldn't go and buy the present, so my uncle bought one for me.

Disjunctive pronouns (page 60)

1
a él, b mí, c con nosotros, d A él, e ella, f ti

2

a Es importante tener una novia <u>en la cual</u> tener confianza.
b Ellos son los amigos <u>para los cuales</u> hice tantos esfuerzos.
c Es la casa <u>en la que</u> nací.
d Eres la persona <u>con la que</u> escojo pasar mi vida.
e Vimos al hombre <u>al que</u> habíamos dado el dinero.
f Ayudamos a una niña <u>a la que</u> habían operado.

3

a Es menos importante preguntar qué pueden hacer por nosotros…
b que preguntar qué podemos hacer por ellos.
c Hay agencias en las que pueden confiar.
d Para mí es lo más difícil.
e Hay situaciones en las cuales es fácil meterse…
f pero de las cuales es muy difícil salir.

Mixed practice

Mixed practice (page 61)

1

a i Le regalaron una bolsa de fruta. **ii** La regalaron. **iii** Se la regalaron.
b i Nos contaron la historia. **ii** Nos la contaron.
c i Me hizo una paella. / Hizo una paella para mí. **ii** La hizo. **iii** Me la hizo. / La hizo para mí.

2

a es, **b** van, **c** estás, **d** he, **e** somos

3

a P – detuvo, I – participaba, **b** P – obligó, I – se reunían, **c** P – quisieron, I – mantenía, **d** P – informó, I – maltrataba, **e** P – fue, I – pasaba

4

Preterite: *detuvo* arrested, *obligó* forced, *quisieron* tried (wanted), *informó* reported, *fue* was
Imperfect: *participaba* was taking part in, *reunían* were gathering, *mantenía* kept, *maltrataba* were mistreating, *pasaba* was passing

Mixed practice (page 62)

5

a ocuparon, **b** fueron, **c** prefirieron, **d** salió, **e** sonrió, dijo, **f** murió, **g** detuvo

6

a I wanted to go out with my wife to go for tapas.
b We were walking down the street looking for a tapas bar.
c There were at least fifty people in each bar.
d Apparently it is a very popular neighbourhood.
e I wanted to call a restaurant to make a reservation.
f Unfortunately my phone wasn't working.
g So my wife made the call for me.

8

a Es muy importante saber que las regiones de España tienen su propia identidad.
b A veces la identidad local es más fuerte que la identidad nacional.
c Lo más imprescindible es contar con instituciones en las cuales puedes confiar.
d Es menos fácil confiar en una institución de Madrid.
e Es bueno tener a alguien a quien echar la culpa.

Mixed practice (page 63)

9

a mí, **b** nosotros, **c** conmigo, **d** nosotros, **e** la nuestra, **f** Lo, **g** Le, **h** ti

10

a Normalmente, **b** lenta y elegantemente, **c** bien, **d** demasiado, **e** mejor, **f** individualmente

11

a Mi madre quiere que vengas a cenar.
b No me importa si vienes o no.
c Preferiría salir.
d Puedes decidir qué decirle.
e No le digas que es mi idea.
f No le he dicho nada.
g No creo que sepa.

Mixed practice (page 64)

12 and 13

	presente – yo	pretérito – yo	pretérito – él	imperfecto – yo	participio pasado	futuro – él
ser	**soy**	**fui**	**fue**	**era**	sido	será
hacer	**hago**	**hice**	**hizo**	hacía	**hecho**	**hará**
volver	**vuelvo**	volví	volvió	volvía	**vuelto**	volverá
morir	**muero**	morí	**murió**	moría	**muerto**	morirá
ir	**voy**	**fui**	**fue**	**iba**	ido	irá
conocer	**conozco**	conocí	conoció	conocía	conocido	conocerá
estar	**estoy**	**estuve**	**estuvo**	estaba	estado	estará
decir	**digo**	**dije**	**dijo**	decía	**dicho**	**dirá**
hablar	hablo	hablé	habló	hablaba	hablado	hablará
comer	como	comí	comió	comía	comido	comerá

14
a introdujo, **b** dijeron, **c** mantengo, **d** han descubierto,
e impusieron, **f** preferiría, **g** vi, **h** paseaba, **i** jugué

Translation practice: Spanish to English (page 65)

1
a large, **b** carry on, **c** engage in, **d** the policeman, **e** cliché, **f** of
course, **g** it caused, damage

2
a Do you know where they are from?
b I have some friends I can meet up with.
c The majority of Spanish people usually go to bed very late.
d According to what my mum says, I don't sleep enough.
e Thirty young people took part in the protest.

3
a Instead of going to bed, I went out partying.
b It made the girl very sad. / It caused the girl a lot of sadness.
c Before arriving we ate something.
d I find that boring.
e My teacher is very good at running.
f I am interested in studying.

Translation: Spanish to English (page 66)

4
The region of La Mancha is known for three things. They are:
the ingenious knight Don Quijote, Manchego cheese, and
the film director Pedro Almodóvar. Of course, you have to
know about more than just these three popular clichés, but
if you do know them, you already know something about
La Mancha. You know its isolated towns, its landscape, its
windmills. You are aware of its traditions and beliefs. You can
guess at the life of the shepherd and the rigours of migrating
with the sheep. And you respect the ingenuity (and genius)
of its inhabitants.

5
The Spanish are thinking of getting rid of the siesta. Having
a rest in the afternoon means wasted hours which then
forces them to stay at work until nine at night. The majority
of workers don't have the opportunity to return home to take
advantage of their two free hours at midday. Working until
nine means having dinner at ten and watching television
until midnight. Twenty-five per cent of Spanish people admit
to routinely going to bed after midnight.

6
Thirty young people who took part in an antifascist protest
were arrested by several police officers of the National Police.
They had forced them to return to the Plaza de España
square, which led to the confrontation. Bottles and stones
were thrown at the patrol cars and they caused serious
damage to street furniture, such as rubbish bins set on fire,
litter bins pulled up or broken bus shelters. According to
what a spokesperson explained, the action of the police at all
times followed the aim of protecting the Falange (right wing
party) demonstration which had been authorised and in
which some three hundred young people participated.

Translation practice: English to Spanish (page 67)

1
a arquitectura, **b** arqueología, **c** tecnología, **d** inmigración,
e habitantes, **f** darse cuenta, **g** segundo, **h** inaceptable, **i** el
alcalde, **j** responsable, **k** apariencia, **l** población

2
a una demostración, **b** una manifestación, **c** pacífica,
d tranquila, **e** el policía, **f** la policía

3
a hagas, **b** hace, **c** sea, **d** es, **e** piense, **f** piensa

4
a sabe, **b** conocen, **c** encontrarme, **d** conocieron, **e** encontrar,
f reconoció, **g** te des cuenta, **h** somos conscientes

Translation practice: English to Spanish (page 68)

5
Todos sabemos cuáles son los tópicos de la cultura andaluza.
Pero por supuesto todos nos damos cuenta de que hay más
que conocer. Es ridículo que pienses que todos los habitantes
se pasen el tiempo tocando la guitarra o escuchando a
Paco Peña. No es una región que viva en el pasado. De
hecho el emplazamiento arqueológico más antiguo de
España, Marroquíes Bajos en Jaén, se ha convertido en una
urbanización.

6
La siesta es un tópico de la vida de los españoles.
Tradicionalmente el día se ha dividido en dos, con cinco
horas de trabajo por la mañana, y luego, después de una
comida y una siesta, una vuelta al trabajo a menudo hasta
las ocho o las nueve de la noche. Significa que cuando la
mayoría de los trabajadores de otros países están saliendo
del trabajo a eso de las cinco de la tarde, los españoles están
empezando la segunda parte del día.

7
Una protesta de jóvenes que se manifestaban contra la
inmigración ha sido dispersada por la Policía Nacional.
La manifestación no era violenta, pero no contaba con la
autorización oficial. Un portavoz aseguró que la policía no
tienen en cuenta las opiniones que se expresan, en la medida
en que se mantengan dentro de la legalidad. En este caso
no se realizó ninguna detención dado que los manifestantes
negociaron con la policía y se dispersaron de buena voluntad.
El alcalde ha dicho que es inaceptable que tales protestas se
permitan, pero la policía dice que si se otorga el permiso, una
protesta pacífica podría tener lugar.

Section 4

The subjunctive of futurity (page 69)

1
i *Voy a España* refers to a habitual action. Every time I go to
Spain.
ii Subjunctive of futurity. *Cuando vaya* referring to an action
which has not yet happened and might not happen.

2

a When they have finished the restoration, it will be a most important work of art.

b As soon as he/she arrives, tell him/her to call me

c When you go to Granada, you will have to visit the Alhambra.

d The day you get married, I promise to be there.

e Until he/she pays, he/she won't be able to come in.

f After they go, we'll clean the house.

3

a vamos, b vaya, c entra, d venga, e nieve

4

a Cuando tenga treinta años …

b Cuando vaya a Argentina …

c En cuanto tenga mi propia casa …

d El día que acabe del instituto …

e En cuanto compres un ordenador nuevo …

f Cuando las mujeres tengan los mismos derechos … second half of the sentence has to refer to the future

Expressions followed by the subjunctive (page 70)

1

a i *para* + infinitive, no other person involved

a ii *para que* + subjunctive – in order for someone else to do something

b i *sin que* + subjunctive – without someone else doing something

b ii *sin* + infinitive, no other person involved

c i past tense *fue* indicates a past completed action

c ii *vayas* indicates a future event which may not happen

d i *haya* indicates a future event which may not even happen

d ii this use of *después de* and infinitive followed by future tense indicates a future action

2

a vaya, b hagamos, c explique, d envíe

3

a Spain will always be a monarchy, unless some scandal happens.

b We make sacrifices in order that our children have a better life.

c We are going to do it without them telling us how to do it.

d Before it is too late, we have to act now.

4

a Para que los niños enfermos puedan sobrevivir, estamos pidiendo dinero.

b Antes de que se acabe el programa, apunta este número.

c A menos que tengas una idea mejor, no iremos.

d Con tal de que nos ayude, todo saldrá bien.

e No podemos hacerlo sin que nos apoye.

The imperfect subjunctive (page 71)

1

a I, b S, c S, d I, e S, f I, g S

2

a olvidaras, b sacarais, c fuera, d apoyaras, e dijeran

3

a ayudaran/ayudasen, b hiciéramos/hiciesemos, c fuera/fuese, d sufriera/sufriese, e dijera/dijese

The imperfect subjunctive with *if* (page 72)

1

a iii, b ii, c iv, d i, e v

2

a pasaría, estuviera

b ocurriría, cometiera

c vieras, apoyarías

d enfrentara, haría

4

a If I had the money, I would go to Spain.

b If I went to Spain, I would stay in a luxury hotel.

c If I stayed in a luxury hotel, I would eat in the restaurant.

d If I ate in the restaurant, I would try tapas.

e If I tried tapas, I would like them a lot.

f If I liked them, I would be happy.

The pluperfect subjunctive (page 73)

1

hubiera salido, hubiera pasado, hubieran sacado a la luz, hubiera podido

2

Other sentences are possible but these are suggested:

a iii If the country had had a strong king, there wouldn't have been a war.

b vi If my grandma hadn't married my grandfather, I wouldn't have been born.

c ii If we had known, we wouldn't have bought that horse.

d v If they had won the match, they would have won the league.

e i If it weren't for the rain we would have had a perfect holiday.

f iv If you had called, I wouldn't have been waiting for you.

3

a If the King hadn't called the Generals, they would have put tanks onto the streets of Madrid.

b If General Armada had been at the Palace, he would have supported the coup.

c If they had punished Tejero after Operación Galaxia, he wouldn't have been able to take part in the coup.

d If the army had waited, the government would have fallen.

Sequence of tenses (page 74)

1

a formarás un gobierno, formas un gobierno, forma un gobierno

b escribirás una carta, escribes una carta, escribe una carta

2

a i If we don't help, the children will die.

b iii If we didn't help, the children would die.

c ii If we hadn't helped, the children would have died.

d vi If the King didn't act, democracy would fall. (would have fallen is also possible)

e iv If the King hadn't intervened, democracy would have fallen.

f v If the King does nothing, democracy falls.

3

a iii, **b** iii, **c** i, **d** ii, **e** iv

Stress (page 75)

a ex**a**men
b ex**á**menes
c organizaci**ó**n
d organizaci**o**nes
e jard**í**n
f jard**i**nes
g ir**é**
h ir**e**mos
i ju**e**go
j jug**a**mos
k si**e**te
l set**e**nta

2

a *Joven* ends in *-n*, so the stress is on the first syllable. When you make it plural an accent is needed to keep the stress in the same place.

b The future tense has the stress on the endings, but *-emos* has the stress in the right place without the need for an accent.

c *Obligación* ends in *-n* so it needs an accent to put the stress on the last syllable. In the plural it ends in *-s* so the stress falls on the *-on* without the need for an accent.

d These are different words: public, I publish, he published

3

a jóvenes, querían, autoridades, cambiaran, exámenes
b había, árboles, jardín, público, que
c si, queréis, podéis, mostrárselas, más
d Pondremos, números, telefónicos
e mi, móvil, Dámelo
f Dónde, está, papá

Mixed practice

Mixed practice (page 76)

1

a quieren que sea
c cuando llegue
e irían
g para que no provocara
h que los niños murieran
i que dejaran
j hubiera matado

2

Si el rey hubiera apoyado el golpe, hubiera llamado a los capitanes generales para decirles que asaltaran las Cortes. Los capitanes generales hubieran sacado los tanques a las calles. La democracia hubiera caído. Se hubiera impuesto un gobierno militar.

3

Students write their own answers using the conditional, conditional perfect or pluperfect subjunctive.

Mixed practice (page 77)

4

a Who would have imagined that a forty year old woman, mother of two children, would want to fight in the bullring?
b If it were not for a good cause, it would be unbelievable.
c If it wasn't a woman, would it surprise us as much?
d How can you stand up for women's rights, ignoring the rights of animals?

5

a quisiera, **b** lidiara, **c** volviera, **d** habría, **e** fuera, **f** hiciera

6

Cristina Sánchez has decided to return to bullfighting one more time. She wants to raise money for Doctor Luis Madero's Foundation for children who suffer from cancer. Many people tried to persuade her not to do it. Her husband suggested asking their children, thinking that it would scare them so much they would say no. But they were very excited by the idea, and this was the decisive factor.

Mixed practice (page 78)

8

organizada, después de, tapándose, algunas, él, contratado, traído, dijo, se pague

9

a pasaría, pudiera
b podrías, decidieras
c tuvieras, irías
d escogieras, tendría
e ocurriría, ignoraras
f les gustaría, vinieras

10

a Cuando hayan completado el aeropuerto, ¿tendrán pasajeros?
b En cuanto llegue el ministro, empezarán a gritar.
c Después de que se vaya, hablarán con la prensa.
d Hasta que cambie de parecer, seguiremos protestando.
e Cuando va a España siempre vuela.

Mixed practice (page 79)

11

a Pensaba que era peligroso.
b Quería que los ayudáramos.
c No pensé que fuera tan malo.
d Querían que cambiara de opinión.
e Fue imposible que hicieras algo.

f A los jóvenes no les interesaba cambiar nada.
g Los jóvenes querían cambiar el mundo.

12

a *Agua* is feminine but takes *el* because it begins with a stressed *a*. Use *estar* for temporary state.

b *El policía* means the policeman. Translate *quiso* as 'tried'.

c Subjunctive of futurity. *Háblele* needs an accent to keep the stress in the right place. *Le* is the indirect object pronoun, 'to him/her'. The *hable* is the subjunctive for an imperative to *usted*.

d *Había vuelto* is the pluperfect with an irregular past participle. *Volver a* means to do something again. 'It had started to rain again.'

e *Tuvieras* is imperfect subjunctive, 'if you were to have'. *Otro* doesn't need an article in front of it. *Tampoco* can start a sentence without the need for a *no*.

f *Sus* can mean 'his/her/their'. *Se* can mean 'each other' as well as 'themselves'. *Antes de* + noun.

13

a The president could have controlled the armed forces.

b It is a scandal that they have denied that the massacre took place.

c If it were not for the courage of the bishop, nobody would have known anything about what happened.

d It is even more shocking that he was killed.

Translation practice: Spanish to English (page 80)

1
a i, **b** ii, **c** iii, **d** v, **e** iii, **f** iv, **g** ii, **h** i, **i** iv, **j** i

2
a charitable foundation, a charity, a not-for-profit body
b to raise funds, to collect money, to make money

3
a A charitable foundation has been set up to raise funds for good causes.
b That organisation has made a total of 300,000 euros in just three months.
c The amount of money collected is much greater than what was expected when the charity was launched.

4
a **ii** immunity, **b** **iv** prerogative, **c** **v** compensation, **d** **iii** to deprive, **e** **i** right

Translation practice: Spanish to English (page 81)

5
Speaking two or three languages is something completely normal. In many regions of Spain it is not a surprise that young people, as well as learning two foreign languages, speak another language either at home or at school, which is a joint official language along with Spanish in their autonomous community. Sometimes it is a mother tongue for children who are already bilingual, but for quite a large percentage of pupils, going to school means studying in another language. Imagine learning algebra in a language you are learning.

6
David Ortiz is a baseball player born in the Dominican Republic. His nickname is Big Papi. He has established a trust that raises money to help children who need a heart operation. He uses his contacts in the world of sport to organise golf tournaments to bring in money for his charity. In 2008 he launched a wine label with his image on, which made a hundred and fifty thousand dollars.

7
The King is immune from prosecution, but under the law nobody can be deprived of his rights even if another person were to have the prerogative. In the unlikely case that the King were to commit a crime, the judge would have to investigate the facts. At this stage of the legal process, the immunity of the King would have no effect whatsoever. From the moment where the King's responsibility was established, nobody would be able to take action against him. But it does not mean that he could avoid the responsibility or the payment of any compensation set out by the judge. It seems incredible that this is the case, but that is what the Constitution sets out.

Translation practice: English to Spanish (page 82)

1
a Madrid, **b** madrileños, **c** madridistas, **d** español, **e** noroeste, **f** son, **g** idioma

2
a me, **b** mí, **c** mi, **d** mí, **e** conmigo, **f** mí

3
a Si tuviera el dinero, iría a España.
b Si tuviéramos la oportunidad, ayudaríamos a otros.
c Si tuviera el tiempo, haría trabajo de voluntario.
d Si cometiera un delito, sería detenido.
e Si ese fuera el caso, sería inaceptable.
f Sería mucho mejor si fuera posible.
g Si no les dieran comida a los pobres, los ricos tendrían que comerse el dinero.

Translation practice: English to Spanish (page 83)

4
El idioma que llamamos 'español' también se llama 'castellano' para diferenciarse de las otras lenguas que se hablan en España. Los otros idiomas también son oficiales en su comunidad autónoma respectiva. El gallego y el catalán no se consideran dialectos; son idiomas derivados, con el transcurso de los años, del latín. El euskera o vascuence es un idioma de origen desconocido, completamente distinto de cualquier otro idioma europeo actual.

5

Cada vez que veo a los niños a los que hemos ayudado, y veo que vienen corriendo hacia mí, a abrazarme y a darme las gracias, me olvido de la fama y el dinero, y pienso en mis propios hijos. Pienso en que sería de mí si estuviera enfrentándome a la misma situación con un niño así y si no tuviera la oportunidad de poder hacer nada por él. Eso es lo que me motiva a hacerlo.

6

Imagina que el rey cometiera un crimen, ¿sería procesado? La pregunta es extraña pero la respuesta es bastante clara. El rey cuenta con inviolabilidad frente a la fiscalía. Lo he comentado con colegas y hemos llegado a la conclusión de que las entidades/los órganos legales españolas/españoles no podrían actuar, aunque en el caso de algunos delitos identificados por la Corte Penal Internacional, un proceso podría iniciarse. Tendría que encontrar un jurista entre un millón para dar con una opinión diferente.